Suffering
and the
Christian Life

Richard W. Miller, editor

ORBIS BOOKS

Maryknoll, New York 10545

Founded in 1970, Orbis Books endeavors to publish works that enlighten the mind, nourish the spirit, and challenge the conscience. The publishing arm of the Maryknoll Fathers and Brothers, Orbis seeks to explore the global dimensions of the Christian faith and mission, to invite dialogue with diverse cultures and religious traditions, and to serve the cause of reconciliation and peace. The books published reflect the views of their authors and do not represent the official position of the Maryknoll Society. To learn more about Maryknoll and Orbis Books, please visit our website at www.maryknollsociety.org.

Published by Orbis Books, Maryknoll, New York 10545-0302.

Manufactured in the United States of America.
Manuscript editing and typesetting by Joan Weber Laflamme.

Library of Congress Cataloging-in-Publication Data

Harrington, Daniel J.
    Suffering and the Christian life / Daniel J. Harrington, S.J., M. Dennis Hamm, S.J., Susan A. Calef, Richard W. Miller, Michael J. Himes, Elizabeth A. Dreyer ; edited by Richard W. Miller.
        pages cm
    ISBN 978-1-62698-013-6 (pbk.)
    1. Suffering—Religious aspects—Christianity. 2. Suffering—Biblical teaching. 3. Christian life—Catholic authors. I. Miller, Richard W., II. II. Title.

BV4909.H368 2013
231'.8—dc23

                                                                2012033156

Contents

Introduction

Richard W. Miller

Suffering is inescapable for human beings and touches the core of their existence and self-understanding. The experience of suffering for Christians is interpreted through their belief in a loving God who is intimately involved with them. In the face of suffering Christians can feel that this God of closeness has abandoned them. Suffering then raises many questions: Why do we suffer? Where is God in our suffering? Who is this God that allows us to suffer? Where is God's purpose in our suffering? While the negativity of suffering creates such quandaries for the Christian, the Christian tradition has also viewed suffering in positive terms. Jesus' suffering has been seen as salvific; indeed, his followers are called (in Mark, Matthew, and Luke) to take up their cross and follow him. This collection of essays responds to the myriad problems that emerge for the Christian in the face of suffering by drawing upon the wisdom of the scriptures and contemporary reflection in order to explore the problem of suffering and the meaning and significance of suffering in Christian life.

The first part of the book (the first three essays) focuses on the Bible as a deep and rich resource for dealing with the reality and theology of suffering. In the first essay, "Old Testament Approaches to Suffering," Daniel J. Harrington, SJ, examines five approaches to suffering in the Old Testament: the lament psalms, the law of retribution, the mystery of suffering, redemptive suffering, and the apocalyptic solution. In the second part of his essay he moves from general observations of approaches to suffering in the Jewish scriptures to a close reading of Psalm 22, which might be the most familiar of the biblical laments. The first words of this psalm—"My God, my God, why have you forsaken me?"— were the final words of Jesus before he died on the cross. Harrington's analysis of Psalm 22 helps us understand the psalmist and also sets the stage for interpreting Jesus' death in the two essays in this volume on suffering in the New Testament.

In the second essay, "The Sharing of His Sufferings: The Social Cost of Following Jesus," M. Dennis Hamm, SJ, explores the New Testament teaching on the meaning of Jesus' suffering and the suffering of Jesus' disciples. Fr. Hamm first examines a selection of New Testament texts, and then he analyzes in depth Paul's letter to the Philippians, which interprets Christ's suffering through the lens of the self-emptying of Christ. The authors of the New Testament are not interested in the classic philosophical problem: Why does a good and all-powerful God allow his creatures to suffer? Rather, the New Testament authors are mainly interested in *apostolic* suffering—the suffering consequent upon the conduct of one's mission. For Jesus, that means the suffering that followed from his obedience to his mission from the Father. For followers of Jesus, that means the suffering that is a side effect of following Jesus in a world hostile to his way. In the New Testament, Christian suffering is the predictable outcome of living the way of life that Jesus models and advocates.

While Fr. Hamm focuses on Paul, especially Paul's letter to the Philippians, Dr. Susan A. Calef focuses on Mark in the third essay—"Taking Up the Cross: Suffering and Discipleship in the Gospel of Mark." Mark is central to the New Testament understanding of suffering because it is the earliest Gospel, and as such is a major source of the perspectives found in Matthew and Luke. In addition, Mark is central to the questions of this book because Mark focuses both on the meaning of the cross and the relationship between Jesus and his disciples. Mark affords access to a deep and rich vein of wisdom to be mined for theological reflection on suffering and Christian discipleship. Jesus' invitation to the disciples to "take up your cross and follow me" (Mk 8:34) has often been interpreted as a call to see any and all suffering in one's life as one's cross to bear. Dr. Calef argues that this interpretation has been harmful, even deadly, for women and groups subject to power structures that marginalize and subordinate them, as numerous feminist and liberation theologians have argued in their critiques of traditional theologies of the cross. Cognizant of the feminist critique, Dr. Calef first clarifies the original meaning of the invitation to take up one's cross and follow Christ by attending to its historical, cultural, and narrative contexts. Second, she offers several clarifications of the meaning of suffering in Mark, including arguments that the Gospel of Mark does not claim that God wills suffering, that suffering (in and of itself) is a good for us, or that suffering itself (including Jesus' suffering) somehow saves. Third, she outlines the Markan understanding of Jesus' messianic suffering and its implications in our contemporary context for the messianic community of disciples.

Part II (the last three essays) draws upon scripture, doctrine, and human experience to reflect on the experience of suffering in Christian life. In the fourth essay, "The Divine Purpose and Human Suffering," Richard W. Miller first argues that the proper theological response to the problem of reconciling human suffering with the Christian belief in a God of infinite wisdom, power, and goodness is not to try to solve the unsolvable, but to preserve the mystery of God. Second, in light of the mystery of God and the concomitant limits to human knowledge, Dr. Miller formulates the most foundational or most basic question for further reflection regarding the problem of human suffering and belief in a God of infinite wisdom, goodness, and power; namely, if God created the universe in order to give God's self to creatures so that they could be united with God and share in the fullness of God's life, could God have achieved this purpose without *any* suffering of created persons? Dr. Miller then responds to this foundational question through an examination of created freedom in relationship to the created person's end. Finally, he shows how the conclusions from the analysis of the freedom of created persons relates to the problem of human suffering from nature (tsunamis, plagues, etc.) and the question of God intervening (special divine action) to prevent human suffering.

In the fifth essay, "The Suffering of Christ," Michael J. Himes reflects upon Jesus' suffering and what it means to say that Jesus' suffering redeems us. First, Fr. Himes examines the meaning of suffering and argues that suffering is not simply pain but rather the experience of pain as out of one's control. As such, suffering is intimately related to the experience of absolute dependence that we experience as finite creatures. Second, Fr. Himes reflects upon Jesus' suffering. Jesus' agony is not physical pain; it is the seeming purposelessness of his approaching death and the possibility of despair that opens before him. In light of this understanding of suffering and its application to Jesus' suffering, he then reflects upon how Jesus' suffering redeems us.

In the sixth and final essay, "Suffering in Christian Life and Experience," Elizabeth A. Dreyer distinguishes the multitude of uses for the word *suffering* and reflects upon the challenge of finding meaning in suffering. Dr. Dreyer examines the personal and global contexts of suffering, distinguishes various types of suffering, and identifies seven themes related to suffering that are particularly relevant and pressing for our time: the evil of suffering in itself; various images of God created in response to the problem of suffering; the call to alleviate suffering; the importance of prophetic witness; loss and grief; prayer and ritual; and hope. In terms of hope she concludes that the Christian God takes human suffering seriously, to the point of entering into it with compassion, love, and courage, and thus transforming it through the power of the Spirit.

PART I

BIBLICAL THEMES CONCERNING SUFFERING

ONE

OLD TESTAMENT APPROACHES TO SUFFERING

Daniel J. Harrington, SJ

Suffering is a universal human experience. Taking it as a starting point for theology makes us face a genuine human problem and challenges us to relate theology to experience and experience to theology. What we are now considering is, I believe, very important. What is suffering? To suffer is to undergo or feel pain or distress; to sustain injury, disadvantage or loss; or to undergo a penalty or punishment. In the midst of suffering most of us feel isolated or alone. We ask "Why me?" And we find ourselves dissatisfied with the usual answers. I grew up in a very Irish family. In our living room we had a plaque on the wall that reminded us, "Things are never so bad that they can't be worse." That counts as Irish optimism. We react to suffering in various ways: resistance, flight, rationalization, prayer, transforming it into a positive experience, or even shopping.

There is no single answer in the Bible to the problem of suffering; there is no "one size fits all" approach. In fact, no answer is totally satisfying to those in the midst of suffering. Rather, the Old Testament presents us with a variety of perspectives, any one of which may be helpful in a time of crisis or chronic suffering. But, of course, sometimes nothing makes sense out of suffering, at least from our limited human perspective. However, there is much wisdom in the Old Testament's approaches to suffering. Without them we cannot understand Jesus or the New Testament.

The Old Testament is an especially rich resource for dealing with the reality and theology of suffering. My task is to provide a brief survey of the various approaches to suffering in what is 75–80 percent of the Christian Bible. In this chapter I want first to explore five approaches to suffering in the Old Testament: the lament psalms, the law of retribution, the mystery of suffering, redemptive suffering, and the apocalyptic solution. Then I want to focus on a particular text, Psalm 22, and use it as the occasion to reflect on some biblical perspectives about suffering.

Five Old Testament Approaches to Suffering

Lament Psalms: The Voice of Those Who Suffer

In my opinion the most important contribution that the Old Testament can make to the theme of suffering in Christian life and experience comes in the lament psalms. Among the 150 psalms in the Book of Psalms the largest category is the lament. Perhaps as many as one-third of the psalms can be classified as laments. They can be either personal or communal. They are basically prayers in which suffering individuals or suffering communities bring before God the pain or hurt they feel and ask God to do something about it. The most famous of the biblical laments is Psalm 22, whose first words, according to Mark and Matthew, were the last words of Jesus: "My God, my God, why have you forsaken me?"

The biblical laments follow something of a script. There are five major elements. First, there is an address to God, marking the psalm as a dialogue and a prayer. Second, there is the lament or complaint itself; that is, the material in which the person or community describes what the problem is or was (danger from drowning, sickness, threats from enemies, and so on). The vagueness of most descriptions is made up for by their high emotional level. Their vagueness also allows us to use these psalms some twenty-five-hundred years after their original composition. Third, there is a confession or profession of trust in God, based mainly on what God has done in the past. Often there is also a challenge to the effect that here and now God's honor is at stake and so God should do something about it. Fourth, there is the petition, the explicit request that God move into action and do something about the situation. Fifth, and last, there is usually an indication that God has indeed answered that prayer, or at least an expression of hope and trust that God will do so. While these five items do not always come in the same order or receive the same emphasis, in most biblical laments they are present.

Psalm 3 is a short and simple example of a lament. The psalmist addresses God directly ("O Lord"), complains that he has many enemies who are claiming that God is no help to him, professes his trust in God as a shield, asks God to strike down his enemies, and concludes that "deliverance belongs to the Lord." In his petition he begs that God might strike his enemies on the cheek and break their teeth.

While the biblical laments may not always reach the high ethical level of the Sermon on the Mount, they can and do help suffering persons get in touch with the intensity of their feelings and express them in no uncertain terms. Moreover, they can help suffering persons to recognize that they are not alone in their suffering, and that in fact they stand in solidarity with others in a whole tradition of suffering persons. These psalms also manage to raise the hard theological questions: Why am I suffering? Why isn't God doing anything about it? Finally, most of the biblical laments end on a note of deliverance or hope, thus conveying the message that suffering does not have the last word. The biblical laments do not answer all our questions. In fact, they are more interested in the "how" of suffering than in the "why."

Mainline Theology: The Law of Retribution

The most common Old Testament answer to the question Why do we suffer? is the law of retribution. According to this principle, acts have consequences. Wise and righteous persons are rewarded, and foolish and wicked persons are punished. In other words, we get what we deserve. The usual assumption in most of the Old Testament is that rewards and punishments take place in this life, not after death. Life after death in the earlier parts of the Old Testament (including most of the psalms) is a shadowy and unhappy existence in an underworld called Sheol (see Psalm 88 and Job 3 for descriptions of this dismal state).

In the Torah, the first five books of the Old Testament, wise and righteous behavior means fulfilling the various commandments in the Jewish Law. In Deuteronomy 30, Moses promises Israel that if *they* choose life and keep the commandments they will become numerous and will prosper, and warns them that if they fail to do so they will perish. The great Old Testament prophets (Isaiah, Jeremiah, Ezekiel) never tire of blaming the misfortunes of Israel, and especially the destruction of Jerusalem and its Temple in the sixth century BCE, on the sins of the people. But they also promise that if the people mend their ways, things will go well for them. The sages behind the Book of Proverbs insist repeatedly on the "law" of retribution. For example, "the integrity of the upright guides them, but the crookedness of the treacherous destroys them" (Prov 11:3).

While the law of retribution is the most common approach to suffering in the Old Testament, there are variations and criticisms of it. According to Genesis 3, the effects of the "original sin" of Adam and Eve extend to all of humankind in all generations. And in Joshua 7, Achan's sin of taking some spoils of battle meant for dedication to God brought God's anger on the whole people of Israel. On the other hand, the prophet Ezekiel argues strongly (chap. 18) against the concept of inherited guilt, that is, against the idea that the sins of the fathers are visited upon their children. And the wisdom teacher known as Ecclesiastes in Greek and Qoheleth in Hebrew expresses skepticism about the validity of this so-called law. He reports in 7:15 that "there are righteous people who perish in their righteousness, and there are wicked people who prolong their life in their evil-doing." For him, death is the great equalizer. He says that "the same fate comes to all, the righteous and the wicked" (9:2).

Suffering as a Mystery: The Book of Job

The most sustained and challenging exploration of the problem of suffering in the Bible is the Book of Job. It examines how one can hold together the three propositions that God is omnipotent, that God is just, and that innocent persons like Job can and do suffer. This is often called the problem of theodicy, literally trying to justify the ways of God especially with regard to apparently innocent suffering.

In the prose narrative that begins the Book of Job (chaps. 1—2) we meet Job, who is a model of righteousness and fear of the Lord. When suffering comes upon him, he submits courageously at first. There he is the patient Job. His patience, however, wears thin very quickly; in chapter 3 Job curses the night of his conception and the day of his birth and repeatedly asks why he has to go on living. There ensues a series of debates between Job and his alleged friends (chaps. 4—37). His friends insist that Job must have sinned (otherwise he would not be suffering), while Job points an accusing finger at God and questions the justice of God. Then God speaks from the whirlwind and effectively puts Job in his place as a creature of God (chaps. 38—41). In chapter 42, Job relents and apologizes for his boldness. Finally, God vindicates Job over against his friends and restores his family and possessions twofold.

Like most great literature, the Book of Job is ambiguous and admits of different interpretations. The book does not solve the problem of innocent suffering; rather, it explores the problem of theodicy. It reveals the inadequacy of some of the conventional solutions, especially the law of retribution. It shows the inadequacy of imposing a legal framework and the rules of human (retributive) justice on God in the area of suffering. It promotes a respectful silence (fear of the Lord) in the face of the mystery of suffering, and a spiritual transformation by which we try to view the cosmos and humans' place in it from God's perspective rather than our own all-too-human one.

Redemptive Suffering: The Servant of the Lord

To call suffering redemptive means that the enduring of suffering by one person or group can have a positive effect on and for other persons or groups. People sometimes say that this firefighter or that soldier "did not die in vain," implying that the person's death has had or will have some positive result for others. This is the idea behind early Christian professions of faith that say that Christ died "for us" or "for our sins," that is, that Jesus' passion and death brought about forgiveness of our sins and made possible a new and better relationship with God. While not a prominent theme in the Old Testament, redemptive suffering does appear very significantly in Isaiah 53, the last and greatest of the four so-called Servant Songs. No discussion of suffering in the Christian Bible can ignore this text.

This Servant Song is part of a collection of hymns or poems written around 538 BCE to encourage the Judean exiles in Babylon to return home to Jerusalem. It is the high point in Second Isaiah (chaps. 40—55), which is arguably the high point of the entire Old Testament from the perspectives of literature and theology. Its point is that Israel has suffered double for its sins (the cause of the exile, in the poet's mind), and now is the time to start over as the people of God. They do so in large part because of the Servant of the Lord.

Four passages in Isaiah 40—55 (42:1–9; 49:1–13; 50:4–11; 52:13—53:12) refer to a mysterious figure called the Servant of the Lord. Whether he was an individual (a prophet, leader, poet, Moses figure) or a group (the exiled community in Babylon, a group within it, a symbol for Israel as a whole) has been debated for centuries. It is very likely that Jesus related his own sufferings to those attributed to the Old Testament Servant of the Lord and so viewed his own suffering as redemptive. The identification of Jesus with the Servant recurs throughout the Gospels and elsewhere in the New Testament (especially in Acts and 1 Peter).

Here our focus is on the redemptive suffering of the Servant of the Lord according to Isaiah 53. In what sounds something like a chorus, the "many" (presumably Israel in exile, or perhaps the nations of the world) acknowledge that the Servant "has borne our infirmities and carried our diseases . . . was wounded for our transgressions, crushed for our iniquities" (Is 53:4–5). Nevertheless, they also affirm that the punishment inflicted upon the Servant "made us whole and by his bruises we are healed" (53:6). Near the end of the poem God proclaims that "the righteous one, my servant, shall make many righteous, and he shall bear their iniquities" (53:11). The theme of the redemptive suffering of the Servant of the Lord closes the poem: "He bore the sin of many, and made intercession for the transgressors" (53:12).

Justice Deferred: The Apocalyptic Solution

Earlier on, with regard to the Book of Job, I spoke about the problem of theodicy, that is, the problem of trying to hold together three propositions: (1) God is all powerful or omnipotent, (2) God is just, and (3) innocent persons such as Job can and do suffer. The problem of theodicy does not go away easily. I don't know about you. But when things go wrong for me, I instinctively ask, "Why me?" Sometimes I find the answer quickly, in my own carelessness or foolishness; thus, the law of retribution works in such cases. But at other times there seems to be no apparent reason, and I (like Job) begin to wonder about either the omnipotence of God or the justice of God.

Relatively late in ancient Israel's history (and shortly before Jesus' time) there emerged an approach to personal and communal suffering that deferred the definitive display of God's omnipotence and justice until life after death, resurrection, the last judgment, and the full coming of the kingdom of God. This is what we pray for when we say, "Hallowed be thy name, thy kingdom come, thy will be done on earth as it is in heaven."

This approach is called the apocalyptic or eschatological solution because it appears in some of the late revelatory writings in the Bible and related books. For example, the sketch of Near Eastern history from the sixth to the second century BCE in Daniel 11—12 reaches its climax with the resurrection of the dead, the final judgment, and appropriate rewards and punishments: "Many of those who sleep in the dust of the earth shall awake, some to everlasting life and some to shame and everlasting contempt"(Dan 12:2). In 2 Maccabees 7 in several of the dialogues between the wicked king and the seven brothers and their mother, there is talk about resurrection of the body and eternal happiness with God for the righteous martyrs and terrible punishments for the wicked king after their deaths. And in a text read at many Catholic funerals these days, the Book of Wisdom promises that "the souls of the righteous are in the hand of God, and no torment will ever touch them" (3:1).

In all three cases those wise and righteous persons who are suffering in the present are promised vindication in the future, after death, with the full coming of God's kingdom. The idea is that God is omnipotent and God is just. But God's omnipotence and justice will be fully manifest only at the last judgment. In the present, then, we are urged to regard our innocent sufferings as part of the divine discipline by which we become wiser and stronger: "My child, do not despise the Lord's discipline or be weary of his reproof, for the Lord reproves the one he loves as a father the son in whom he delights" (Prov 3:11–12).

In summary, the Old Testament teaches us to look upon our sufferings perhaps as just punishment for our sins, as a mystery, as possibly redemptive in some way, or as a divine discipline. Above all, it teaches us to use the biblical lament psalms for the language, the solidarity, the source of questions, and the hope that they provide so abundantly. And remember always that as people of the Bible we are a community of suffering persons and a community of hope in God's power.

Psalm 22: A Plea for Deliverance from Suffering and Hostility

Rather than continue making general observations about approaches to suffering in the Old Testament, now I want to engage in a close reading of Psalm 22. This is perhaps the most famous and familiar of the biblical laments. According to Mark and Matthew, its first words were the last words of Jesus on the cross. Careful attention to the text as it appears in the New Revised Standard Version illustrates concretely the structure and literary conventions of the lament psalms and brings out their theological significance.

The musical directives that preface Psalm 22—"To the leader: according to The Deer of the Dawn"—and many other Old Testament psalms remain a mystery to scholars. Who "the leader" was, and what "the Deer of the Dawn" meant, we will probably never know. This psalm, like many others, is attributed to David. The ascription most likely reflects a program of making links between individual psalms and events in David's life.

The language of this psalm (and most others) is open and metaphorical, thus allowing many readers over the centuries to identify with its words. In that respect it is something like a Hallmark greeting card that can be used by all kinds of persons in all kinds of situations and still convey a personal and appropriate message to its recipient. That is one reason why we can still recite and pray Psalm 22 some twenty-five-hundred years after its composition.

> ¹ My God, my God, why have you forsaken me?
>   Why are you so far from helping me, from the
>   words of my groaning?
> ² O my God, I cry by day, but you do not answer;
>   and by night, but find no rest.

The opening verses in the psalm identify it as a prayer in direct address to God. The invocation "my God" appears three times, indicating that the psalmist wants to say something important to God. Here the psalmist complains that God has not been paying attention to his repeated efforts to make God listen, and so he feels that God has abandoned him. Nevertheless, he keeps on praying, presumably because he believes that God will eventually hear his complaints. These words, according to Mark 15:34 and Matthew 27:46, are the last words of Jesus on the cross. They can hardly be the despairing cry of an existentialist hero. That would reduce the Gospels to absurdity. Rather, they are a signal that we should read the whole of Psalm 22 and interpret it in terms not only of Jesus' suffering and death, but also of his resurrection and vindication.

Thus he stands in solidarity with all suffering people for whom death does not have the last word.

> [3] Yet you are holy,
>   enthroned on the praises of Israel.
> [4] In you our ancestors trusted;
>   they trusted, and you delivered them.
> [5] To you they cried, and were saved;
>   in you they trusted, and were not put to shame.

The profession of trust in God is an essential element in the script of the biblical laments. In verses 3–5 the psalmist acknowledges God as the Holy One who is worthy of all praises and recalls what God has done for his ancestors in the past. Here he is most likely alluding to the Exodus, when God answered the prayers of the Israelites enslaved in Egypt. The triple repetition of the word *trusted* links the trust shown by Moses and the ancestors and what the psalmist recognizes as what is necessary for himself if his prayer is to be heard by God the Holy One of Israel.

> [6] But I am a worm, and not human;
>   scorned by others, and despised by the people.
> [7] All who see me mock at me;
>   they make mouths at me, they shake their
>   heads;
> [8] 'Commit your cause to the Lord; let him
>   deliver—
>   let him rescue the one in whom he delights!'

The second section of complaint in verses 6–8 focuses on the psalmist's plight. While the language is graphic and emotional, it is not precise enough to let us know what exactly the problem was. At any rate, he feels subhuman, in fact like "a worm." Moreover, his enemies (whoever they may be) are mocking him and making fun of him. They are using his plight to mock Yahweh the God of Israel and are challenging God to rescue his suffering servant. At the same time, the psalmist is subtly reminding God that his suffering is reflecting badly on God and indeed putting God to shame. In other words, God's reputation and honor are at stake in failing to rescue his servant. Echoes of this section appear in the Markan and Matthean passion narratives (see Mk 15:29; Mt 27:39, 43), where Jesus is mocked by the bystanders at the cross.

> [9] Yet it was you who took me from the womb;
>   you kept me safe on my mother's breast.
> [10] On you I was cast from my birth,
>   and since my mother bore me you have been
>   my God.
> [11] Do not be far from me,
>   for trouble is near
>   and there is no one to help.

In the second section about trust in God, the psalmist appeals to his personal experience of God's care for him. In the process of his birth (always a dangerous matter in antiquity) God kept him safe and nourished him from his mother's breast. From the very beginning of his life he has trusted in God and has not been disappointed. Now when he is in deep trouble and there is no one else to help, he asks God to be close to him again, and rescue him. Again we do not know exactly what the "trouble" was.

> [12] Many bulls encircle me,
>   strong bulls of Bashan surround me;
> [13] they open wide their mouths at me,
>   like a ravening and roaring lion.
>
> [14] I am poured out like water,
>   and all my bones are out of joint;
>   my heart is like wax;
>   it is melted within my breast;
> [15] my mouth is dried up like a potsherd,
>   and my tongue sticks to my jaws;
>   you lay me in the dust of death.

Now in verses 12–15 and 16–18 we get two more sections devoted to complaints or laments. Each section begins with animal imagery and moves to the psalmist's complaints about his own intense physical sufferings. In the first segment his enemies are described in verse 14 as "strong bulls" who roar like lions and so are terrifying the psalmist in his suffering. Then in verses 15–16 he uses first-person singular language to describe graphically how bad he feels with regard to parts of his body: his bones (they are out of joint), his heart (it is melted like wax), his mouth (it is all dried up), and his tongue (it is sticking to his jaws). In short, he feels as if he is close to death.

> [16] For dogs are all around me;
>   a company of evildoers encircles me.
>   My hands and feet have shriveled
> [17] I can count all my bones.
>   They stare and gloat over me;
> [18] they divide my clothes among themselves,
>   and for my clothing they cast lots.

In verse 16 the second section begins by comparing the opponents with dogs. In this culture dogs were not pets. Rather, they were wild and generally hungry animals, and as scavengers they were to be feared by humans. Then in verse 16c–17a the psalmist turns again to his own dismal bodily condition: his hands and feet are shriveled up, and his bones are sticking out. In verse 18 his enemies continue to mock him and gloat over him, and even cast lots for his garments. See Mark 15:24 for an echo of this detail in the case of Jesus' crucifixion.

> [19] But you, O Lord, do not be far away!
>   O my help, come quickly to my aid!
> [20] Deliver my soul from the sword,
>   my life from the power of the dog!
> [21] Save me from the mouth of the lion!

After the alternating sections of lament and confession in 22:1–11 and the two further blocks of lament in 22:12–18, the psalmist finally comes to express his petition in verses 19–21a. The preceding material has the effect of clarifying the relationship between God and the psalmist. God has proved faithful both in Israel's history and in the psalmist's life. And the psalmist knows how small and insignificant he is before God. Thus he displays the biblical virtue of fear of the Lord. He knows his place in the schema of creation.

What started as a prayer with the invocations to "my God" at the very beginning of the psalm now reaches its turning point in the explicit request for divine help. The God who seemed so far away is now asked to become close and bring assistance. The psalmist's prayer for deliverance picks up on the animal imagery in the previous sections: "the power of the dog" and "the mouth of the lion." His plight seems to be a matter of life and death: "deliver my soul from the sword."

> From the horns of the wild oxen you have
> rescued me.
> [22] I will tell of your name to my brothers and
> sisters;
> in the midst of the congregation I will praise
> you:
> [23] You who fear the Lord, praise him!
> All you offspring of Jacob, glorify him;
> stand in awe of him, all you offspring of Israel!
> [24] For he did not despise or abhor
> the affliction of the afflicted;
> he did not hide his face from me,
> but heard when I cried to him.

Something dramatic seems to have happened: "From the horns of the wild oxen you have rescued me." The mood of the psalm has changed radically from gloom and despair to vindication and celebration. Most of the lament psalms contain this dynamic in one form or another. Scholars have speculated that perhaps this feature reflects the use of these psalms in the thanksgiving rituals held at the Jerusalem Temple. The idea would be that the initial laments and professions of trust belong to the time before the rescue or healing and that the final comments are made when the crisis is over and the psalmist has offered or is offering a thanksgiving sacrifice. The biblical notion of thanksgiving involves stating publicly that God is the one responsible for the rescue or healing. The thanksgiving sacrifice might also entail a celebratory meal at the Temple, at which the remains of the animals being sacrificed might provide food for the one making the sacrifice and his guests.

In the second part of Psalm 22 the psalmist invites the participation of his family (22:22–24), a larger congregation (22:23–24), and the whole world (22:27–31) in what seems like a celebratory meal. In addressing first his "brothers and sisters" he gives testimony that God has indeed answered his prayer and urges them to join him in praising and thanking God. He calls on those who "fear the Lord" to praise God. Fear of the Lord in the Old Testament means knowing who God is and who you are. This recognition, of course, is basic to the dynamic of the whole psalm.

> [25] From you comes my praise in the great con-
>   gregation;
>   my vows I will pay before those who fear him.
> [26] The poor shall eat and be satisfied;
>   those who seek him shall praise the Lord.
>   May your hearts live forever!

The psalmist seems so happy that he wants to invite a much larger crowd to his party, even and especially the "poor." The reference to "my vows" probably alludes to the psalmist's promise made in the midst of his trouble that if God did rescue him, he would offer a thanksgiving sacrifice to God.

> [27] All the ends of the earth shall remember
>   and turn to the Lord;
>   and all the families of the nations
>   shall worship before him.
> [28] For dominion belongs to the Lord,
>   and he rules over the nations.

²⁹ To him, indeed, shall all who sleep in the earth
    bow down;
  before him shall bow all who go down to the
    dust,
  and I shall live for him.
³⁰ Posterity will serve him;
  future generations will be told about the Lord,
³¹ and proclaim his deliverance to a people yet
    unborn,
  saying that he has done it.

The psalmist's happiness becomes even more expansive in verses 27–31, so much so that he now invites the whole world to acknowledge and worship the God of Israel. He affirms the absolute sovereignty of God and wants all the ends of the earth to join him in the celebration of praise and thanksgiving. Indeed, his expansiveness grows in verses 29–31 to include both those who have died and those who are yet unborn. The English translation of verse 29 in the NRSV is probably clearer than the Hebrew text warrants. But it is hard to escape a reference to the dead being alive enough and conscious enough to join in the thanks and praise. Compare the description of the abode of the dead (Sheol) in Psalm 88:10–12, where Sheol is the "land of forgetfulness" and there no one can praise God. Here the dead "shall live for him" (God), and future generations will say "he [God] has done it"—the perfect expression of thanksgiving in the Bible.

Psalm 22 illustrates the literary structure and conventions of the biblical lament. It addresses God directly. It lodges a series of complaints or laments. It also contains professions of trust in God's power to save. It reaches a climax with a petition for God's help in verses 19–21a. It ends in verses 21b-31 with an elaborate and inclusive thanksgiving. Its open and metaphorical language means that it can be (and has been) used on many occasions and by many different persons, including Jesus of Nazareth at the moment of his death on the cross, according to Mark and Matthew. Throughout the centuries it has encouraged suffering persons to ask the hard theological questions, to express their pain, to connect with the community of suffering persons, and to find hope in the midst of their suffering. Suffering does not have the last word. In my view, Psalm 22 expresses well the greatest contributions of the Old Testament to our topic of suffering in Christian life and experience.

TWO

THE SHARING OF HIS SUFFERINGS

The Social Cost of Following Jesus

M. Dennis Hamm, SJ

When the authors of the New Testament writings speak of the sufferings of Jesus and of Christian disciples, there is no evidence that they are interested in the classic philosophical problem of pain. That is, they do not deal with the question, Why does a good and all-powerful God allow his creatures to suffer? Rather, the New Testament authors are mainly interested in what I will call *apostolic* suffering—the suffering that is consequent upon pursuing a God-given mission. Regarding Jesus, that means the rejection he experienced as a result of his prophetic proclamation of the reign of God, a rejection that finally culminated in his execution by Roman crucifixion. And for Jesus' followers—especially after his death, resurrection, and Pentecost—it was the suffering that is the inevitable side effect of continuing Jesus' mission in a world hostile to his way. For the New Testament authors Christian suffering is the predictable, even inevitable, outcome of living the way of life that Jesus models and advocates. It is a consequence of Christian life and mission.

The interest of the New Testament gospel and letter writers is not in the pain but in the shame. Mel Gibson's film "The Passion of the Christ" offers some surprising help in seeing this. Despite its flaws, one clear value of the film is that Gibson's preoccupation with the physical violence and pain of the passion forced the question: Does the director's focus on the physical suffering

of Jesus accurately represent the interest and emphasis of the narratives of the gospel writers and the reflections of the New Testament letters? I submit that their interest lies elsewhere. When they
speak of the suffering of Jesus—and also the suffering of Christian
disciples—it is not the intensity or length of the physical pain that
matters most; rather, for Matthew, Mark, Luke, John, Paul, Peter,
and the author of the letter to the Hebrews, it is *the rejection and
humiliation* that characterize the suffering of Jesus and his followers. The good news, of course, is that this suffering entails joy in
this life and glory in the next.

This essay has two parts. First, I explore a sampling of New
Testament statements about suffering to examine what the earliest
Christian authors actually say about suffering. Second, I explore
more fully Paul's letter to the Philippians, because that short letter
has so much to say about the self-emptying of Christ as both an interpretation of his suffering and as a model for Christian disciples.

The Suffering of Jesus and His Followers

When it comes to the *scourging* (which took some seven excruci-
ating minutes in Gibson's film), the New Testament writers show
great restraint. Mark and Matthew simply mention the scourging
with a participle: "So Pilate, wishing to satisfy the crowd, released
Barabbas to them and, after he had Jesus scourged [*phragellōsas,*
"scourging"], handed him over to be crucified" (Mk 15:15; and
Mt 27:26).[1] Luke quotes Pilate twice as *intending* to have Jesus
flogged and released (Lk 22:16, 22) but does not narrate the flogging. Only John actually narrates the scourging, and he does so
with single word, "Then Pilate took Jesus and had him scourged
[*emastigōsen*]" (Jn 19:1).

The gospel writers treat the *crucifixion* itself with similar brev-
ity, with little attention paid to the obvious pain entailed. "Then
they crucified him," says Mark (15:25). And the other three are
equally brief. For their audiences there was no need to elaborate.
They were familiar with the ritual of Roman execution. For them,
the shame was more significant than the pain. The cultural history
of the Roman Empire helps us understand that crucifixion itself

was the Roman Empire's way of utterly disrespecting, humiliating, and dismissing in the most visible and public way a noncitizen who was judged an enemy of Roman law and order, typically a runaway slave. Crucifixion worked as a deterrent. (Do what this man did and you will end up like this!) Hence, the public venue, hence the tablet naming the crime and the protocol of carrying the crosspiece through the streets to the execution site.[2]

Carrying the Cross

The noncitizen convict was made to carry the crosspiece through the street to the place of execution, not as a matter of Roman convenience but as a shaming ritual. Under the authority of the Roman overlords, bystanders were welcome to heap upon the convict whatever act of humiliation they cared to offer: spitting, vilification, mockery. We catch the spirit of this in the gospel writers' description of the mockery that began with the members of the Sanhedrin, continued with the soldiers in the praetorium, and was sustained by the passersby and Jewish and Roman functionaries under the cross. Down with rebellion! Up with the *pax Romana*, reinforced by proper violence! When Jesus told his followers, "Whoever desires to come after me, must deny himself, take up his cross and follow me" (Mk 8:32; Mt 16:24; Lk 9:23, which exhort one to take up one's cross *daily*), he was making a metaphor of this Roman prelude to crucifixion. Following him meant submitting to a humiliation and rejection that would be like that of the convict carrying the crosspiece through the streets to the upright post waiting for him at the execution site. Notice that the focus is on *carrying* the cross, not on getting crucified.[3]

The Synoptic Passion Predictions

That crucifixion was more about humiliation than physical pain also comes through in the passion predictions in the Synoptic Gospels. Mark's version sets the pattern. Jesus "began to teach them that the Son of Man must suffer greatly and be rejected by the elders, the chief priests, and the scribes, and be killed, and rise after three days" (8:31). The emphasis is on rejection, which can be read as an elaboration on the nature of the suffering. "To be rejected" here translates a Greek word that is more specific than its rough equivalent in English, "reject," that is, *apodokimasthēnai*, which carries the sense of rejection that follows upon an evaluative examination. And in this context this deliberate rejection is performed by the highest religious and imperial authorities of the land. The third prediction (Mk 10:33) further elaborates the humiliation aspect of the first, this time adverting to a double handing over and highlighting the Romans' part in the shaming: "Behold, we are going up to Jerusalem, and the Son of Man will be handed over to the chief priests and the scribes, and they will condemn him to death and hand him over to the Gentiles who will mock him, spit upon him, scourge him, and put him to death, but after three days he will rise." Perhaps the strongest expression of crucifixion as denigration and shaming is the question that the Markan Jesus asks in the conversation with Peter, James, and John after the transfiguration: "How is it written regarding the Son of Man that he must suffer greatly and be *treated with contempt?*" (Mk 9:12).[4]

Hebrews 12:2

A summary verse from the letter to the Hebrews (12:2b) provides further evidence that crucifixion was understood essentially as a shaming device: "For the sake of the joy that lay before him he endured the cross, despising its shame, and has taken his seat at the right of the throne of God."

Another sign that the suffering of crucifixion was considered mainly as denigration is that the *opposite* of suffering in the New Testament is never simply relief, recovery, or healing; the opposite of the suffering of cross bearing and crucifixion is glory and/or vindication. The previous quotation from Hebrews 12 is an example of that understanding. The mention of resurrection as the climax of the three synoptic passion predictions is further evidence. First comes the denigration, then the exaltation.

The Last Beatitude and Prophetic Suffering

Besides the saying about carrying the cross, another key saying of Jesus regarding the suffering of disciples is the last beatitude (Mt 5:10–12; Lk 6:22–23). Listen to Matthew's version, the eighth beatitude and its two-verse elaboration:

> [10] Blessed are they who are persecuted for the sake of righteousness, for theirs is the kingdom of heaven.
> [11] Blessed are you [plural] when they insult you and persecute you and utter every kind of evil against you [falsely] because of me.
> [12] Rejoice and be glad, for your reward will be great in heaven. Thus they persecuted the prophets who were before you.

As we will see, persecution is one of the main ways followers of Jesus suffer. To be persecuted for the sake of righteousness is to be persecuted for doing God's will, "righteousness" meaning, in this case, doing the right thing in the context of one's covenant relationship with God and others. In verse 11, the shift from the third-person discourse to the second plural—you—makes explicit that it is the followers of Jesus, disciples of every age, who are addressed. Persecution is again named as what the blessed suffer, but the three other verbs in this verse indicate that persecution is of a piece with insult, reproach, and vilification. Then the consequence of the eighth beatitude—"for theirs is the kingdom of God"—is paraphrased as "for your reward will be great in heaven." Verse 12, then, provides a surprising interpretation of what is going on in this suffering. It is because Christian disciples are functioning *like the Israelite prophets of the past* that they will be rewarded. In other words, Christian suffering is apostolic because it is prophetic. It is because they are persecuted as exponents of the word of God that they are insulted, reproached, and vilified, and like the prophets of old, they will also be rewarded by God. As in the references to Jesus' suffering, exaltation follows humiliation. Christian suffering, then, is a predictable consequence of acting like the earlier prophets.

Apostolic Suffering: A Cluster of Themes

Besides being a key expression in Jesus' teaching on the nature of Christian suffering, the last beatitude entails a cluster of themes that recurs in all of the major documents of the New Testament when their authors narrate or address examples of Christian suffering:

- Christian suffering is usually a matter of *shaming (*mostly verbal but often physical).
- Christian suffering is *apostolic*, or *evangelical*, in that it is both intended by the sufferers and perceived by the perpetrators as done "in the name of the Lord"; as such, it advances the gospel. Such suffering marks the sufferer as a prophet in that he or she speaks in the name of God. This suffering is therefore considered an *honor* rather than a shame.
- *Joy* is mentioned either as a spontaneous consequence or as a divine reward or affirmation of Christian suffering.
- Christian suffering *imitates the life of Jesus Christ* (though not explicit in the last beatitude, this is implied by the context of the Beatitudes in the narrative of the Gospels).
- Therefore, the Christian becomes an *example for others*.
- Christian suffering is *inevitable* (implicit in Synoptic Gospels; explicit in John, Acts, Peter, and Paul).
- Suffering Christians experience themselves *sustained by the Holy Spirit* or by *the Father* or *the presence and power of the risen Jesus*, even as they are afflicted.

It is fascinating how elements of this cluster show up in certain summary passages in a variety of New Testament documents.

Acts 5:17–41

When Peter and the apostles were brought before the Sanhedrin, after the angel of the Lord released them from prison and they were found in the temple area teaching the people, they preached the gospel to the assembly and finished with the words, "We are witnesses of these things, as is the Holy Spirit that God has given to those who obey him." After Gamaliel makes his wait-and-see case to his peers, the Sanhedrin recalls the apostles, has them flogged, orders them to stop speaking in the name of Jesus, and dismisses them. Luke writes:

> So they left the presence of the Sanhedrin, rejoicing that they had been found worthy to suffer dishonor [*katēxiōthēnai . . . atimasthēnai*] for the sake of the name. And all day long both at the temple and in their homes, they did not stop teaching and proclaiming the Messiah, Jesus.

Note the cluster of themes: They are *empowered* by the Holy Spirit. They are imprisoned precisely *as a consequence of preaching the gospel*. They *rejoice* after the flogging. Imprisonment and getting flogged are interpreted as suffering *dishonor* [*atimasthēnai*], which they, however, now consider an *honor*. Dishonored by men, they are honored by God. Their mindset is clearly different from the world around them. There is no focus on the pain, which was surely a factor in the flogging.

Acts 14:22

After Paul and Barnabas were expelled from Pisidian Antioch and then suffered an attempted stoning in Iconium, Jews from Antioch and Iconium turn up at Lystra and successfully stone Paul and drag him out of the city, supposing that he is dead. However, after evangelizing Derbe, Paul and Barnabas *go back through the sites of persecution*—Lystra, Iconium, and Pisidian Antioch. Luke writes, "They strengthened the spirits of the disciples and exhorted them to persevere in the faith, saying, 'It is necessary for us to undergo many hardships to enter the kingdom of God'" (Acts 14:22). What is striking here is that the undergoing of "hardships" (*thlpseis,* "afflictions" or "tribulations") is considered a God-given necessity [*dei*, the Lukan word for divine necessity].[5]

2 Timothy 3:10–12

Apparently, the apostolic suffering that occurred in this first missionary journey of Paul and Barnabas became emblematic of any Christian's suffering, for 2 Timothy treats the apostolic sufferings of this mission as iconic:

> You have followed my teaching, way of life, purpose, faith, patience, love, endurance, persecutions, and sufferings, such as happened to me in Antioch, Iconium, and Lystra, persecutions that I endured. Yet from all these things the Lord delivered me. *In fact, all who want to live religiously in Christ will be persecuted.* (2 Tm 3:10–12, emphasis added).

Colossians 1:24

Even this brief review of the New Testament treatment of Christian suffering cannot bypass the problematic statement of Paul regarding his own suffering (as "making up what is lacking in the afflictions of Christ") in the first chapter of his letter to the Colossians:[6]

> [24] Now I rejoice in my sufferings [*pathēmasin*] for your sake, and in my flesh I am filling up what is lacking [*antanaplērō to hysterēmata*] in the afflictions of Christ [*tōn thlipseōn tou Christou*, literally "the afflictions of the Messiah"] on behalf of his body, which is the church, [25] of which I am a minister in accordance with God's stewardship given to me to bring to completion [*plērōsai*] for you the word of God, [26] the mystery hidden from ages and from generations past. But now it has been manifested to his holy ones, [27] to whom God chose to make known the riches of the glory of this mystery *among the Gentiles*; it is *Christ in you* [or "Messiah among you (plural)"], the hope for glory. [28] It is he whom we proclaim, admonishing everyone and teaching everyone with all wisdom, that we may present everyone perfect in Christ. [29] For this I labor and struggle, in accord with the exercise of his power working within me. (emphasis added)

Although it is the clause "I am filling up what is lacking in the afflictions of Christ" that cries out for explanation, I quote the six verses of this passage because they make up a single sentence in the Greek and provide the necessary context for understanding the troubling clause.

What is problematic about verse 24, of course, is the apparent assertion that something was lacking in the redemptive suffering of Christ, a notion that goes counter to the main point of the whole letter, namely, that the Colossian Christians have no need for the faith and practices of the "seductive philosophy" that some would impose upon them (2:6–23); on the contrary, they have in Christ the incarnate Son all the redemptive mediation they could possibly need (1:15–23). Is there, then, an understanding of verse 24 that fits more coherently with the rest of the letter? Yes, there is. First, "the *afflictions* of Christ" translates a word—*thlipseis*—which is not used elsewhere in the New Testament to refer to the sufferings that Jesus endured in his passion and death (those sufferings are called *pathēmata*). *Thlipseis*, on the other hand, is a word that almost always refers to the persecutions long associated with the Jewish end-time expectation of troubles that would come with the advent of the Messiah. These troubles or afflictions are usually rendered in English as "tribulations." And since "Christ" in this verse comes with the definite article, *tou Christou* can be rendered literally as "of the Messiah." So "the tribulations of the Messiah" can easily be understood, as it has been by a number of exegetes, as "the messianic woes."

Second, another unusual word calls for attention, the one translated "I make up"—*antanaplērō,* which occurs only here in the New Testament. It is made of three parts: (1) *plēroō,* a common word meaning "to fill," (2) *ana-*, a prefix heightening the meaning, so that *anaplēroō* means "fulfill," or "complete," or "occupy," and (3) *ant-,* another prefix, this one carrying a relational note—sometimes of reciprocity, sometimes of replacement. Thus *antanaplērō* means "take one's turn in filling up something."[7]

So Paul can be read as saying what could be rendered in English as "I take my place in completing what is lacking in the messianic afflictions." In other words, "The sufferings entailed in my imprisonment are something I joyfully endure as an inevitable side effect of our share in the mission of the Messiah, our risen Lord Jesus." He is considering his part in the end-time plan of the Father, who has "delivered us from the power of darkness and transferred us to the kingdom of his beloved Son" (1:13). The rest of the single sentence underlying verses 24–28 touches on the rest of that plan, which includes "bringing to completion" the word of God, including revelation of the surprising mystery of "the [Jewish] *Messiah among you* [Gentiles!]." And so this passage in Colossians coheres not only with the rest of the letter to Colossians but with the treatment of the suffering of disciples that we find throughout the New Testament.

Paul's Approach to Christian Suffering in His Letter to the Philippians

One key text for studying Paul's understanding of the interface between the sufferings of Jesus and those of Christian disciples is Philippians 3:7–11:

> [7] Yet whatever gains I had, these I have come to regard as loss because of Christ. [8] More than that, I regard everything as loss because of the surpassing value of knowing Christ Jesus my Lord. For his sake I have suffered the loss of all things, and I regard them as rubbish, in order that I may gain Christ [9] and be found in him, not having a righteousness of my own that comes from the law, but one that comes through faith in Christ [*tēn dia pisteōs Christou*; cf. NRSV translation note: "Or *through the faith of Christ*"], the righteousness from God based on faith. [10] I want to know Christ and the power of his resurrection and the sharing of his sufferings [*koinōnian tōn pathēmatōn autou*] by becoming like him [*symmorphizomenos*] in his death, [11] if somehow I may attain the resurrection from the dead.

On first reading, even apart from the context, it is evident that Paul has experienced a transformation of values such that knowing

Jesus as his Messiah and Lord is so good that knowledge of him
and being "in him" (his phrase for being in the body of Christ, the
Christian community) has made everything else pale in compari-
son. Further, this transformation of mindset has changed his way
of understanding what it means to be in right relationship to God
("righteousness"); that relationship is now based not on carrying
out the Pharisaic interpretation of the 613 laws of Moses, but on
a righteousness initiated by God and entailing faith.

But several expressions call for clarification: (1) Is that "righteousness" simply a gift of God, or does it entail Paul's responsive
action? (2) How is that ambiguous Greek phrase *pisteōs Christou*
best translated? Grammatically, the genitive case here can mean either "faith or trust in Christ," where the genitive case is understood
as signaling the object of faith, *or* it can mean the *faithfulness*
that *Jesus* exercised with respect to God the Father. (3) To what
sufferings of Jesus does Paul refer? The physical pains entailed in
the passion of Christ? The ongoing rejection, denial, and betrayal
he experienced throughout his public life, especially at the end?
(4) What does "sharing" in those sufferings mean for Paul? (5)
Is the experience of the power of Christ's resurrection something
accessible in the present life of the church, or is this a reference
to Paul's hope for his own ultimate resurrection? And (6) being
"conformed to [Christ's] death"—is that a desire of Paul to be
literally crucified by the Romans? If not that, what does it mean?

It takes the full context of the letter to begin to answer these
questions. A reading of the whole letter makes it obvious that the
famous hymn about Jesus' self-emptying, Philippians 2:6–11, is
the primary key to Paul's meaning.

Paul's Situation

First, though, we need a sense of Paul's situation as he writes. A
review of the scholarship on this question reveals the following
consensus about Paul's situation as writer. He is in prison (he
refers to his "chains"—translated "imprisonment" in the NAB
version of this letter—four times, 1:7, 13, 14, and 17). Why is he
in chains? The charge of Philippian citizens in Acts 16:20–21 is

a good clue—"These people are Jews and are disturbing our city and are advocating customs that are not lawful for us Romans to adopt and practice." What Paul preaches—claiming that a crucified Jew (claimed to be raised) is Lord of all (*not* the emperor) and that there is an empire that transcends Rome ("the kingdom of God")—this message was interpreted by some as a rebellion against Roman law and order.

Paul's Audience

Who are the Philippians to whom Paul writes while in custody and awaiting trial? Philippi was an important city of some ten thousand people judging from the archeology, in the province of Macedonia. A colony of Rome (that is, a place governed by the same laws as the city of Rome), it was occupied by retired Roman militia and their descendants. It was a highly stratified society, ranging from a minority of wealthy elite, down through farmers and craftsmen, down further to the very poor. Slaves and former slaves made up a significant portion of the community. Slaves, of course, participated in the lifestyle of their owners; they were not among the very poor, since poor families could not afford them, but on the social ladder slaves occupied the bottom rung. The archeological artifacts from this area—many of them memorial plaques celebrating the role and accomplishments of their sponsors—suggest that, next to Rome itself, Philippi may have been the most status-conscious city in the empire. One's place in the "pecking order" of society governed one's sense of self-worth. Since there is no evidence of a synagogue there, Jews (like Lydia and her women friends, mentioned in Acts 16) must have been a tiny minority.[8]

The Christian community, then, was an almost entirely Gentile subgroup, a few hundred perhaps, no doubt representing the spread of the social strata of the town (including some elite, some farmers, merchants and craftsmen, including their slaves, and also the very poor). The members of this subgroup, with their recently acquired Jewish ways, would no doubt be seen as out of step with the Roman program, with their refusal to engage in emperor worship and their clannish gatherings around special meals, songs, and prayer. Many citizens no doubt took their commercial and labor needs to other shops and labor pools.

Paul's Exhortation

To this struggling Christian community Paul writes his encouraging word. His advice is to continue to work for the unity of their little community by continuing to invest themselves in a lifestyle of self-giving, which they already know was established by the grace of God during their initial response to the gospel. Basically that means to imitate the way of Jesus, and also to imitate the lives of those especially touched by that grace. The centerpiece of his persuasion is the famous "Christ hymn" that makes up verses 6–11 of chapter 2, so named because the poetic density, beauty, and structure of the passage is such that it can stand alone as a profound expression of Christian faith. It has invited the speculation that these six verses compose a hymn that fits the picture of the Roman writer Pliny, who observed that Christian groups gathered in the early morning for meals at which they "sang songs to Christ as God." Whether or not Paul here quotes a traditional hymn or wrote the piece himself, it is clear that the passage is the centerpiece around which he builds the whole letter. To hear it properly, we need to take seriously its immediate setting—the nine-verse exhortation that precedes it and the seven-verse application that follows immediately after it.

His exhortation begins with the brilliant imperative: *politeuete*, a verb that means "conduct yourselves," but with the social and civic connotation that carries over into English words with the *polit*-root, such as *politics.* In other words, "With respect to the social world you inhabit, behave as follows." Paul says he wants to hear that they are "standing firm in one spirit, with one mind struggling together [*synathlountes*] for the faith of the gospel, not intimidated [*ptyromenoi*] in any way by your opponents." The first participle carries a robust connotation from the world of sports; the prefix *syn*, of course, means "with," and the *athl*-root we use in *athletics.* So the import is, "struggle together as one, like a team." The participle rendered "intimidated" is a strong word, *ptyrō,* appearing only here in the Bible; the participle can also be translated "terrorized"—which hints at what the Philippians are facing in the behavior of their pagan neighbors. Next we hear, "This is proof [*endeixis,* perhaps better rendered "sign"] to them of destruction, but of your salvation." The meaning of that sentence is best paraphrased as, "Your adversaries among the larger Philippian community take your struggle as a sign of your destruction, but you recognize it as an experience of salvation [*sōtēría*], for your ability to stand firm is the work of the Spirit"; for, as the next sentence puts it, "this is *God's* doing, as *you* know well but your foes don't." Nine verses earlier, Paul had invested that word "salvation" [*sōtēría*] with a special meaning. Considering the two possible results of his incarceration—execution or going free—he quotes Job 13:16, "I know that this will result in *sōtēría* for me." Either way, life or death, he knows that nothing will separate him from Christ.

Paul continues, "For to you has been granted, for the sake of Christ, not only to believe in him but also to suffer [*paschein*] for him." This is the only instance of the verb *paschein* ("to suffer") in this letter, and the context shows that it refers to persecution resulting from their fidelity to the gospel way of life. Resorting again to sports talk, Paul says, "Yours is the same struggle [*agōn,* "match," as in wrestling] as you saw in me and now hear about me." So Paul sees the inconvenience and indignity of his imprisonment for the gospel as a kind of suffering, in which he, too, is sustained by God in the struggle.

That said, Paul moves in chapter 2 to more specific practices that will implement what it means to "stand firm in one spirit and struggle together for the faith of the gospel" (1:27).

> [1] If there is any encouragement in Christ, any solace in love, any participation in the Spirit, any compassion and mercy, [2] complete my joy by being of the same mind [*to auto phronēte*], having the same love, united in heart, thinking one thing [*to hen phronountes*] [3] Do nothing out of selfishness or out of vainglory; rather, humbly [*en tapeinophrosynē*] regard one another [*allēlous hēgoumenoi*] as more important than yourselves, [4] each looking out not for his own interests,

but [also] everyone for those of others. [The Greek words inserted here entail vocabulary that appears in the Christ hymn that follows.]

Although I called this an exhortation about practices, these practices are not physical actions. They are practices of the mind, ways of thinking together about things or persons. It is about fostering a mindset, what the Greeks call a *phronēsis,* from the verb that occurs twice in verse 2 and ten times altogether in this letter. If the audience seeks a concrete example of this mindset, Paul presents it now in the Christ hymn.

The Christ Hymn

Verse 5 makes a bridge: "Have this mindset among yourselves, which [is] also in Christ Jesus" (my translation). Then comes the hymn. The first half, verses 6–8, describes the career of the Messiah Jesus as "downward mobility" from divine supremacy to the depths of solidarity with human suffering, a passage that flies in the face of the typical social ladder climbing celebrated in the Roman colony of Philippi:

> [6] Who, though he was in the form of God [*en morphē theou*],
>> did not regard equality with God something-to-use-for-his-own-advantage [*harpagmon hēgēseto*].[9]
> [7a] Rather, he emptied himself [*auton ekenōsen*],
> [b] taking the form of a slave [*morphēn doulou labōn*]
> [c] coming in human likeness [*en homoiōmeti anthrōpōn genomenos*];
> [d] and found human in appearance [*kai schēmati heuretheis hōs anthropos*],
> [8] he humbled himself [*etapeinōsen heauton*]
> becoming obedient unto death, even death on a cross [*genomenos hypēkoos mechri thanatou,*

> *thanatou de staurou*]. (NAB 1986, except
> for the change in the rendering of *harp-*
> *agmon* to reflect the solution discussed
> below.)

Already, only halfway through the hymn, these words throw light
on some of the meaning of Phil 3:7–11, which was the passage
we began with. It becomes clear what Paul means by "the sufferings of Christ: first, there is the self-chosen letting go of sharing
the form of God. Since God has no form in the ordinary sense,
"form" here must mean something like the visible expression of
being divine, like the manifestation of the divine Son sharing in
the process of creation and the supreme status that comes from
that sovereignty. The self-emptying is best understood as the incarnation, taking on the limitations of human nature, much as the
prologue of John expresses that mystery. The eternal Son takes
on the form of a slave not only in that sense but also in the sense
that his life was that of service ("The Son of man came not to be
served but to serve"). Verse 7cd (coming in human likeness and
being found human in appearance) simply underscores 7ab (rather
he emptied himself . . .) in synonymous parallelism. But verse 8
elaborates on how Christ Jesus lived out that human condition: in
self-humiliation with respect of human beings and in obedience
to God the Father, even unto death.

Scholars sometimes take the phrase "death on a cross" as an
addition to a putative pre-Pauline hymn. That seems to me an
unwarranted speculation, for, given the context of utter self-emptying and humiliation, death by crucifixion comes as the ultimate
denigration. It is the "bottom" to which the downward trajectory
has been pointing all along.[10] The form of execution that was
crucifixion, with its shaming ritual of the carrying of the cross,
reserved only for noncitizens of Rome, was the most extreme form
of disrespect in the Roman Empire's symbolic repertoire. Notice
that Paul, or the putative author of the hymn, makes no mention
here of blood and pain. It is this rejection and degradation that
constitutes for Paul the essence of "the sufferings of Christ." Naming this process "obedience" helps us see that the phrase that the

NAB renders "through faith in Christ" through which righteousness comes from God (3:9) is probably best rendered "through the
faithfulness of Christ." This reading also saves the final phrase of
3:9, "depending on faith," from redundancy.

Finally, the hymn helps us understand what Paul means when
he says, "to know him and the power of his resurrection and
the sharing of his sufferings by *being conformed to his death
[symmorphizomenos tō thanatō autou]*." Apart from the context
that includes the Christ hymn, we might hear this as a desire to
literally be crucified as Jesus was. But with the hymn in the background, with its language of moving from the *morphē* of God to
the *morphē* of a slave, when Paul chooses to create a new word
(occurring only here in the Bible, and for the first time in Greek
literature) with the *morph* root, this must be a deliberate allusion
to those other *morph-* words in the hymn. Then his meaning in
"being *con-formed* to his death" must mean something like taking
on the mindset of Christ as revealed in both the self-emptying of
his incarnation and the humiliation of his earthly service, imitating
his "downward mobility." And the purpose is to create unity in the
Christian community.

Now, to follow the second movement of the hymn:

> [9] Because of this, God greatly exalted
>   [*hyperýpsōsen*] him
>   and bestowed upon him the name that is above
>   every name,
> [10] that at the name of Jesus
>   every knee should bend
>   of those in heaven and on earth and under the
>   earth
> [11] and every tongue confess that
>   Jesus Christ is *Lord*
>   to the glory of God the Father.

Thus what Paul calls "the sufferings of Jesus" come about as a
deliberate self-emptying of the eternal Son, becoming human,
and then humbling himself in the slave-like service of others to

the point of suffering the ultimate denigration of slaves, death by crucifixion. What follows is a divine exaltation that is an extreme reversal of the humiliation. Scholars are surely right to find in this language of humiliation followed by exaltation an allusion to that same movement in Isaiah 53, especially in its Greek version. The Septuagint (the most influential of the Greek versions of the Hebrew Old Testament) rendition of Isaiah 53:13 uses the verb *hypsoō* to speak of God's exaltation of the Servant; Paul alludes to, but trumps, that expression by creating a verb that appears nowhere else in the Greek Bible, *hyper-ypsoō,* or "hyper-exalt," caught in the NAB's "greatly exalted."

"The name that is above every name" that is given to him is not "Jesus," which was the Greek form of a common name for Jewish males named after Joshua. But because of *who* it is who bears the human name in this case, the name of Jesus now exalted evokes universal worship of him as LORD. Thus *Kyrios* ("Lord") is the "name that is above all names." This becomes clear when we recognize in the clause "every knee should bend . . . and every tongue confess" an allusion to another part of Isaiah (45:23), which occurs in a passage that is one of the most powerful expressions of Hebrew monotheism in the scriptures. To quote just part of this oracle:

> Who announced this from the beginning and
>   foretold it from of old?
> Was it not I, the Lord, besides whom there is no
>   other God?
> There is no just and saving God but me.
> Turn to me and be safe,
> all you ends of the earth,
> for I am God; there is no other!
> By myself I swear,
> uttering my just decree and my unalterable word:
> To me every knee shall bend
> by me every tongue shall swear,
> Saying, "Only in the Lord are just deeds and
>   power;

> Before him in shame shall come all who vent
>   their anger against him.
> In the Lord shall be the vindication and the
>   glory of all the descendants of Israel." (Is
>   45:22–25)

All that this passage implies about the name Lord is applied to Jesus in the hymn. But to make sure we hear this in a way that still honors Paul's Jewish monotheism, the hymn ends with "to the glory of God the Father." As in the credo of 1 Corinthians 8:6,[11] we are still in the framework of the *Shema,* honoring God as One. It is important to note that the pattern of denigration followed by exaltation is what we also found in other references to the suffering of Jesus and his disciples: the Synoptic Gospels' passion predictions, in the last beatitude, and throughout Paul's letters.

Paul's Application of the Hymn

What stands at the center of the application that follows the hymn is a sentence so familiar that it has become a kind of Christian maxim: "Work out your salvation in fear and trembling" (2:12b). Most of us probably hear "your" in the second person singular, and we hear it as an exhortation to work for individual perfection so that we can find salvation after death. This understanding is not without merit, but it is inadequate because it does not understand the mandate in its context. The "you" is the same plural "you" Paul has been addressing all along, meaning this audience, the Christians in Philippi. And the "salvation" to which he refers is the same *sōtēría* that he was referring to in the instructions to the community prior to the introduction to the Christ hymn. The sign of salvation in 1:28 is the very power of God supporting them in their "struggling together for the faith of the gospel, not intimidated (or terrified) in any way by [their] opponents." So the task of working out their salvation is not primarily the individual struggle to avoid personal sin, but the living of community life according to the practices of Philippians 2:1–4. These practices include doing nothing out of selfishness or vainglory, and humbly regarding others as more important then themselves, each looking not for his or her own interests but everyone for those of others. This is what is involved in putting on the mind of Christ Jesus as illustrated in his self-emptying, humbling, and humiliating service of others' needs. This is what it means to share in the sufferings of Christ and even to be conformed to his death. The fact that the author creates a neologism in the word rendered "being conformed" *(sym-morphizomenos)*—echoing the two instances in the Christ hymn of *morphē* ("form" in "the form of God" and "the form of a slave")—indicates that he is not speaking of a literal copying of Jesus' death (that is, crucifixion, for which, as a Roman citizen, Paul is not even a candidate). Rather, he is speaking of self-emptying and humbling service in the spirit of Jesus' life and death. The hope for a consequent exaltation—although, again, analogous to, not a literal copy of, Jesus' exaltation (which in his case is a full restoration to his sharing in the "form" of God)—is spelled out by the statement: "That if possible I may attain the resurrection from the dead."

It is important to notice that soon after Paul mentions this shared task of self-emptying to build up the unity of the community, this "working out" of a shared salvation, he hastens to add, "For *God* is the one who, for his good purpose, works [*energōn*] in you [*en hymōn* better, 'among you'] both to desire and to work." So Paul is not urging some kind of Pelagian self-saving or "works righteousness." The church is God's work in progress, with God involved in both the desire and the work; we cooperate.

Paul proceeds to speak of the formation and growth of the Philippian community as also the product of his labor, which he hopes will be his boast on judgment day before Christ, a sentiment he climaxes with a clear reference to the Christ hymn: "But, even if I am *poured out* as a libation upon the sacrificial service of your faith [*epi tē thysia kai leiturgía*]." Given that he is speaking of an extreme possibility ("even if"), he seems to be using the pouring out of wine on the Tamid (the twice-daily atonement sacrifice of the lamb in the Temple) as an image of a possible *getting emptied out*, which seems to be referring to his possible execution by the Romans as a blessing added to their own self-emptying service of one another in the building up of community. This is very much in the spirit of Paul's charge to the Christians in Rome: "Offer your bodies as a living sacrifice, your spiritual worship" (Rom 12:2). This mundane, daily struggle is nothing less than a collective sharing in the suffering of Christ, a being conformed ("sym-*morph*-ed") into his death. In this, the Philippians' struggle to be faithful to Christ and to one another, while enduring the shunning and shaming by their pagan neighbors, is paralleled to Paul's joyful suffering of imprisonment.

Timothy and Epaphroditus

On a quick first reading, one might take what comes next, Paul's news about and comments on Timothy and Epaphroditus, as bits of small talk that he simply wants to include in this letter of friendship. In fact, his commendation of these two companions continues his presentation of examples of living out the mind of Christ. In a situation (Rome, presumably) where many so-called Christians "seek their own interests"—that is, precisely the opposite of the mindset he advocated in the introduction to the hymn (2:4), Timothy stands out as one who has a genuine interest in the concerns of the Philippians. Further, to describe Timothy's collaboration with him in the mission, he uses the word *douleuō*, which means "to conduct oneself as one in total service to another, perform the duties of a slave,"[12] a likely cross-reference to the slave motif of the Christ hymn. Recall that this letter begins by identifying the senders as "Paul and Timothy, slaves of Christ Jesus [*douloi Christou Iēsou*]."

Paul presents Epaphroditus as yet another example of putting on the "mind of Christ." As the Christ hymn spoke of Jesus humbling himself "becoming obedient to the point of death [*mechri thanatou*]" (2:8), so also does Epaphroditus come near to the point of death [*mechri thanatou ēngisen*] for the work of Christ. Further, to characterize the sacrificial nature of this service, Paul returns to the language of temple ritual that he used regarding his own imitation of Christ just eight verses before (his metaphor for possibly being poured out like a libation upon

the Philippians' sacrificial service, *leitourgía*) After commend-
ing Epaphroditus as "brother, co-worker, fellow soldier, your
messenger," he dubs him "[your] *leitourgos* in my need" (2:25).
The same image returns at the end of his commendation: "He
came close to the point of death, risking his life to make up for
the service [*leitourgía*] that you could not perform" (translation
mine). Finally, at the end of the letter, Paul again draws upon the
language of temple sacrifice to refer to the financial aid package
that they sent through Epaphroditus as "'a fragrant aroma,' an
acceptable sacrifice, pleasing to God" (4:18). While the Christ
hymn itself does not employ that language of temple sacrifice,
Paul made the connection in his description of his own and the
Philippians' service at 2:17 and 20.[13]

These commendations of Timothy and Epaphroditus are both
celebrations of men whose suffering is understood as reflecting the
self-emptying of Christ as a consequence of their obedient service
of God the Father.

A Further Personal Reflection from Paul

What comes next, in chapter 3, the famous "beware of the dogs"
passage, is often considered a fragment from some other letter.
Yet this personal reflection of Paul fits into the letter very appro-
priately when seen as still another example of the transformation
of mindset that comes with full conversion to the way of Christ
Jesus.[14] When Paul says, "Writing the same things to you is no
burden for me but is a safeguard for you," it is unlikely that he is
referring to the news that he has just shared regarding Timothy and
Epaphroditus. Rather, he is referring to what he is about to say. For
the topic *is* an old one: the issue of "the Judaizers," about which
he wrote so strongly to the Galatians—the maverick Christian
missionaries who insisted that Gentile converts to the Christian
movement needed to take on the whole Jewish way of life if they
were to be true followers of the (Jewish) Messiah. He now revisits
that issue to show how his own putting on of the mind of Christ
has so transformed him that his being "in Christ" transcends in
value even his beloved Jewish tradition:

> For his sake I have accepted the loss of all things and I
> consider them so much rubbish, that I may gain Christ and
> be found in him, not having any righteousness of my own
> based on the law but that which comes through the faithful-
> ness of Christ, the righteousness from God, depending on
> faith to know him and the power of his resurrection and the
> sharing of his sufferings by being conformed to his death, if
> somehow *I* may attain the resurrection from the dead. (3:8b-
> 11, emphasis added)

Finally, after establishing the context for the statement with which
we began this section, we are ready to hear that language about
knowing Christ "and the power of his resurrection" as referring to
Paul's ongoing experience and that of the Philippians. His ability
to rejoice in the suffering of his imprisonment and the Philippians'
ability to know salvation in God's support as they resisted being
intimidated by their pagan neighbors—these things are in fact
ways of knowing the power of Jesus' resurrection, the experience
of God's righteousness.

The final paragraph of chapter 3 provides two more passages
that further illuminate how Paul uses the Christ hymn as a means
to interpret the Christian experience of faith, hope, and love. As
he has already done twice in this letter, Paul can confidently offer
himself as a model for imitation in this matter of putting on the
mind of Christ: "Join with others in being imitators of me, brothers and sisters, and observe those who thus conduct themselves
according to the model you have in us" (3:17). He is able to do
this without arrogance because he knows his life is evidence of
the power of Christ's resurrection and of God the Father working
among them in both the desire and the working of their community
life. When he says, "For many, as I have often told you and now
tell you even in tears, conduct themselves as enemies of the cross
of Christ," he is not speaking of the pagan neighbors. "The cross of
Christ" is a shorthand reference to the mind of Christ expressed in
the self-emptying service of Jesus unto death on a cross as spelled
out in the Christ hymn. Only "insiders," Christians, could be "enemies of the cross" in that sense. And only fallen-away Christians

are likely to have elicited frequent tears from Paul. He probably means fallen-away Roman Christians on *his* end of this correspondence if he has "often told" the Philippians about them. They are likely the same people he refers to at 2:32, so-called Christians "who seek their own interests, not those of Jesus Christ," and "whose minds are occupied with earthly things" (3:19).

By contrast, he says, "Our citizenship [*politeuma*, also "commonwealth"] is in heaven, and from it we also await a savior, the Lord Jesus Christ" (3:20). In a city that prides itself in being a colony of Rome, and therefore living by the laws of Rome, citizenship is held as a special honor. Paul here reminds the Philippians that while they may be "in Philippi," their real identity lies in being "in Christ Jesus" (see 1:1). Consequently, they await a visit not of Lord *Caesar* but of the Lord *Jesus Christ*—for whom "Lord" is "the name that is above all names" (2:9). Paul further uses language that echoes the hymn when he writes, "He will change [*metaschēmatisei*] our lowly [or humbled] body [*sōma tēs tapeinōseōs,* "body of humiliation"] to conform [*symmorphon*] to his glorified body [*tō sōmati tēs doxēs*] by the power [*energeian*] that enables him also to bring all things into subjection to himself" (3:21). See Philippians 2:13, "It is God who, for his good purpose, works in you both to desire and to work." Thus, for Christian disciples, sharing in the sufferings of Christ entails both being conformed to his death in humble self-emptying and also, finally, the exaltation of being conformed to his risen body. Paul has another way of saying the same thing in the compact statement of 2 Corinthians 4:7–11:

> But we hold this treasure [that is, "the knowledge of the glory of God on the face of Jesus Christ," 4:6] in earthen vessels, that the surpassing power may be of God and not from us. We are afflicted in every way, but not constrained; perplexed, but not driven to despair; persecuted, but not abandoned; struck down, but not destroyed; always carrying about in the body the dying of Jesus, so that the life of Jesus may also be manifested in our body. For we who live are

constantly being given up to death for the sake of Jesus, so
that the life of Jesus may be manifested in our mortal flesh.

"The life of Jesus" is surely the current life of the risen Lord, what
Paul calls in Philippians "the power of his resurrection," accessible
now to Christian disciples in their suffering service.

Final Observations

The New Testament treatment of the topic of Christian suffering
focuses mainly on the suffering that is a consequence of pursuing
a God-given mission. While those effects often entail physical suffering—including imprisonments, hunger, thirst, sleep deprivation,
persecution, whipping, stoning, dangers from travel, rivers, bandits
(2 Cor 11:23–33)[15]—the main emphasis is on the kind of shaming,
humiliation, rejection, and vilification suffered first by Jesus. Taking this reality to heart can free us from the unwarranted fear that
following Jesus necessarily entails an extra load of sickness and
bad luck. This New Testament understanding of suffering may also
keep us from too easily identifying every private injury as an occasion of carrying our cross. On the other hand, taking this theme
seriously can remind us that Christian discipleship calls us to speak
and act like Jesus the rejected prophet, that is, to sometimes speak
and act in ways that challenge the status quo and draw rejection
and humiliation from the world around us.

Jesus' passion, Paul's experience as traveler and frequently
incarcerated missioner, and Stephen's martyrdom inhabit the
Christian imagination as primal examples of apostolic suffering.
However, when it comes to the topic of Christian imitation of
Christ, Paul spends most of his correspondence focusing on the
self-emptying required *to foster and live out the unity of Christian
community*. This is the self-emptying that comes from facing the
daily *internal* challenges of church life—rivalries, pride, mis-
understandings, neglect, moral backsliding, and other lapses in
commitment—along with the challenges external to church life—
cultural shaming, vilification, exclusion, and being ostracized. This

emphasis in Paul's pastoral writing reminds us of the obligation to face and overcome the divisions within particular Christian denominations as well as the hostilities among Christian denominations, and between Christian communities and society at large.

The thesis of this study—that the New Testament portrayal of the suffering of Christ and his followers is mainly focused on the denigration that often accompanies the Christian mission—may come as a disappointment for those seeking in scripture solace for their experience of those *other* sufferings that fill our lives and challenge our faith—sufferings like sickness, financial loss, accidents, and natural disasters. The New Testament's best help regarding this kind of suffering comes, again, from Saint Paul. In response to rival Christian missionaries he names "the super-apostles" (2 Cor 11:5), who boast about their spiritual gifts and visions and apparently challenge Paul's failure to make similar claims, Paul prefers to "boast" of his sufferings in the service of Christ ("If I must boast, I will boast of the things that show my weakness," 2 Cor 11:30). This "boast" climaxes in 2 Corinthians 12:7b-10:

> Therefore, that I might not become too elated, a thorn in the flesh was given to me, an angel of Satan, to beat me, to keep me from being too elated. Three times I begged the Lord about this, that it might leave me, but he said to me, "My grace is sufficient for you, for power is made perfect in weakness." I will rather boast most gladly of my weakness, in order that the power of Christ may dwell with me. There, I am content with weaknesses, insults, hardships, persecutions, and constraints, for the sake of Christ; for when I am weak, then I am strong.

We can only guess what kind of challenge lies behind those two metaphors—"a thorn in the flesh" and "an angel of Satan." The most popular hypothesis among biblical scholars these days is a recurring eye problem (see Gal 4:13–15). Whatever it was, and maybe Paul keeps it vague to make it a generic example for others, several things are clear. The "divine passive"—"was given to me"—indicates that he understands it as coming from God (at least that God allows such suffering). The immediate purpose was to keep Paul "from being too elated" (mentioned twice in the same sentence!); apparently the elation derived from the possibly out-of-body experience and "abundances of revelations" to which he refers in the previous six and a half verses (that is, 2 Cor 12:1b-7). But the subsequent verses add a more positive meaning for this mysterious suffering: it is in his weakness that he best recognizes the power of God the Father and of the Lord Jesus. Even Paul's commentary on physical suffering is related to his apostolic mission, for in the subsequent verses Paul speaks of the "mighty deeds" (healings, no doubt) that accompanied his ministry. And it is his weakness that has helped Paul recognize that the power comes from the Lord.

This brief study helps us see that the New Testament does not supply answers to all our questions about the suffering of Christian disciples. The answers it does provide are surely sufficient, but two millennia of post-biblical experience of the Christian community of faith have provided plenty of further examples and wisdom, not least from those who suffer from addictions like alcoholism, who, after recognizing that they are powerless to save themselves, pray to the "power greater than myself" and then come to experience the liberating power of God.

Notes

1. Unless I indicate otherwise, I am using the New American Bible (NAB) 1986 translation.

2. For a comprehensive survey of the practice and meaning of crucifixion in the ancient world, see Martin Hengel, *Crucifixion in the Ancient World and the Folly of the Message of the Cross* (Philadelphia: Fortress Press, 1977).

3. Hengel notes that the carrying of the cross was a distinct and deliberate part of the punishment: "People were all too aware of what it meant to bear the cross through the city and then to be nailed to it (*patibulum ferat per urbem, deinde offigitur cruci*, Plautus, *Carbonaria*, fr. 2) and feared it" (Hengel, *Crucifixion in the Ancient World and the Folly of the Message of the Cross*, 62).

4. The Greek verb here means literally "to make somebody a nobody."

5. This may well be how Luke understands the difficult-to-translate saying of Jesus at Luke 16:16, "The law and the prophets lasted until John, and everyone who enters it does so with violence [*pas eis autēn biazetai*]."

6. I am aware that many scholars consider Colossians Deutero-Pauline (that is, written in Paul's name after his death by a close disciple), but whether the letter is Paul's or written in his name, the question here is what this statement means as an interpretation of Paul's suffering.

7. This, indeed, is the definition provided in the main lexicon used in New Testament studies today, W. Bauer, F. W. Danker, W. F. Arndt, and F. W. Gingrich, *A Greek-English Lexicon of the New Testament and Other Early Christian Literature,* 3rd ed. (Chicago: University of Chicago Press, 2000).

8. Two valuable studies for reconstructing the social setting of Philippians are Peter Oaks, *Philippians: From People to Letter,* Society for the Study of the New Testament Monograph Series 110 (Cambridge: Cambridge University Press, 2001); and Joseph H. Hellerman, *Reconstructing Honor in Roman Philippi: Carmen Christi as Cursus Pudorum*, Society for the Study of the New Testament Monograph Series 132 (Cambridge: Cambridge University Press, 2005).

9. Recent study of *harpagmon* has found that, when the word appears in the idiom "consider something *harpagmon*," the thing so named is something already possessed, and the owner refuses to treat it as something to be exploited personally. The literature on the meaning of *harpagmon* is vast. A good place to start is Gordon D. Fee, *Pauline Christology: An Exegetical-Theological Study* (Peabody, MA: Hendrickson, 2007), 381–83.

10. Hengel confirms this interpretation: "Death on the cross was the penalty for slaves, as everyone knew; as such it symbolized extreme humiliation, shame and torture. Thus the *thanatou de staurou* ["death on a cross"] is the last bitter consequence of the *morphēn doulou labōn* ["taking on the form of a slave"] and stands in the most abrupt contrast possible with the beginning of the hymn with its description of the divine essence of the pre-existence of the crucified figure, as with the exaltation surpassing anything that might be conceived (*ho theos auton hyperypsōsen*, "God greatly exalted him"). The one who had died the death of a slave was exalted to be Lord of the whole creation and bearer of the divine name Kyrios. If it did not have *thanatou de staurou* at the

end of the first strophe, the hymn would lack its most decisive statement" (*Crucifixion in the Ancient World and the Folly of the Message of the Cross,* 62).

11. "Yet for us there is one God, the Father, from whom all things are and for whom we exist, and one Lord, Jesus Christ, through whom all things are and through whom we exist" (1 Cor 8:6).

12. Bauer, Danker, Arndt, and Gingrich, *A Greek-English Lexicon of the New Testament and Other Early Christian Literature,* under *douleuō.*

13. We have still another example of Paul characterizing financial aid as *leitourgia* at 2 Corinthians 9:12, where he uses the term for the collection of funds for the relief of the poor Jewish Christians in Jerusalem. Thus their financial sacrifice is characterized as the suffering that goes along with discipleship.

14. Indeed, this whole chapter is one of ten units that make up the ten-part chiastic structure that John Heil finds in this letter. See John Heil, *Philippians Let Us Rejoice in Being Conformed to Christ* (Atlanta: Society of Biblical Literature, 2010), 31. As the sixth unit, it functions in the structure as D' and balances with the fourth unit—D 1:19–30. In both of these units Paul presents his own experience as a model for imitation.

15. See also the other three "hardship catalogues" in this letter: 2 Corinthians 4:7–11; 6:4–10; and 12:10.

THREE

TAKING UP THE CROSS

Suffering and Discipleship in the Gospel of Mark

Susan A. Calef

All suffering may be understood as the experience of finitude in tension with intrinsic human dignity. In other words, we humans suffer whenever we experience the limitation and imperfection, whether moral or material, that attend our creaturehood. The fundamental meaning of all loss, injury, and pain, is death, the ultimate limit that challenges the very notion of human dignity.[1] It is this tension between our experience of finitude and our dignity that inspires the questions regarding the cause and meaning of suffering that dog our days and have occupied the minds of philosophers and theologians for generations: Why suffering? Does God will suffering? Dare we conclude that there is a value to individual and collective pain and suffering? What is the appropriate Christian, or more precisely, the appropriate *gospel* response to suffering, our own and that of others? The last question, I suggest, is especially urgent, given our contemporary context: a world in which advanced communication systems and information technology inform us daily of the massive suffering occurring worldwide, and a North American cultural context that encourages us to seek a pain-free life; to avoid, ignore, or deny suffering; to pursue instead a life of hyper-consumerism and the entertainment of spectacle.[2]

Preceding essays in this volume illumine the multiple and rich Old Testament and Pauline traditions on suffering that are precious resources for our ongoing theological reflection on the subject. No discussion on suffering in Christian life and thought, however, would be complete without attention to the experience and praxis of Jesus, which provides the pattern or "way" of our discipleship. This brings us to the Gospels and the story of Jesus, the one to whom we are "discipled." Due to space constraints, rather than attempt to comment on all four Gospels, barely scratching the surface of the rich resources that each affords on the subject, I confine my attention to the Gospel of Mark. As the earliest Gospel, Mark is a major source of the perspectives found in both Matthew and Luke; and of the four Gospels, it is Mark that focuses squarely on Jesus, disciples, and the cross. Therefore, Mark affords access to a deep and rich vein of wisdom to be mined for our discipleship.

As the title suggests, this essay focuses in part on Jesus' invitation to take up the cross and follow him (Mk 8:34). It does so because, in this twenty-first century, theological reflection on suffering in the Christian tradition ought not overlook the critiques and cautions voiced by women, and in particular, the work of feminist theologians and biblical scholars regarding the ways in which our theologies of the cross and preaching about Jesus' suffering have influenced the physical and spiritual lives of women.[3] Like my feminist colleagues in the Academy and the women with whom I interact and share faith in ecclesial settings, I believe that explanations of suffering and of the atonement must be evaluated not solely in light of their conformity to standards of orthodoxy but also in light of their experienced effects, including their impact on the lives of women, past, present, and future. Here I simply summarize women's concerns in this regard, trusting that their relevance for this topic and for our ongoing individual and communal reflection and responses is readily apparent.

In recent decades feminist theologians and biblical scholars have critically analyzed the ways in which masculine God-language[4] and traditional views of God, atonement, suffering, and sacrifice affect women.[5] Of major concern is the particular understanding of the death of Jesus known as the doctrine of penal substitution or satisfaction, which claims that the terrible suffering and death of Jesus were the high price the Son paid to appease the wrath of the Father that had been provoked by humanity's grievous sinfulness. Numerous theologians consider this understanding of Jesus' death deeply problematic.[6] For many, a tradition that glorifies the death of a son whose father wills his suffering or silently stands by while it occurs appears to be a form of divine child abuse. In their classic essay Joanne Carlson Brown and Rebecca Parker conclude, with startling frankness: "Christianity is an abusive theology that glorifies suffering. Is it any wonder that there is so much abuse in modern society when the prominent image or theology of the culture is of 'divine child abuse,'—God the Father demanding and carrying out the suffering and death of his own son?"[7] Such a model, it is argued, with its terrible image of God, has a pernicious effect on how we conceive of divine-human relations as well as human-human relations, not least within families. Those who have walked with a woman trapped in an abusive marriage, listening to her struggle mightily with the burden of guilt that paralyzes her due to her pastor's counsel to bear her "cross" out of love for the abuser and for Christ, who suffered for her, recognize the value of this work by feminist scholars.[8] The uncritical idealization, even valorization, of suffering, self-sacrifice, and obedience as supreme values can have deadly consequences, especially for women and other marginalized persons, for "upholding Jesus' suffering as a model can be twisted into an oppressive tool in a variety of settings, including but hardly limited to sexual abuse. Victims of slavery, racism, unjust wages, torture, human trafficking, and political oppression . . . can all be led to believe that quiet passivity is the appropriate 'Christian' response, for it is one's cross to bear."[9] We may hope that a book such as this will provide the kind of critical, faithful attention—both to the tradition that we cherish and to lived experience—that can transform relational patterns that have proved detrimental to, even deadly for, women and girls around the world.[10]

It is with this potent feminist critique in mind that this essay poses two questions. First, does the Gospel Jesus, and more precisely, the Markan Jesus, call Christians to consider any and all suffering as our personal cross to bear in following him? Second, what can Mark's Gospel contribute to Christian reflection on suffering? In addressing these questions I first clarify the original meaning of Jesus' admonition to "take up your cross" (Mk 8:34) by attention to its narrative, historical, and cultural contexts. I then illumine potential Markan contributions to our theological reflection on suffering by examining the stories of the two characters in the Gospel who are explicitly identified as "suffering many things."

"Take Up Your Cross" (Mark 8:34)

To grasp the original meaning of Jesus' call to "take up your cross" one must attend to its literary and cultural contexts. In terms of its place in the narrative this saying occurs in the central section of Mark's Gospel (8:22—10:52), widely regarded as the gateway to Mark's theological concerns.[11] The section opens with Peter's confession at Caesarea Philippi (8:27–30), where, after first posing the question "Who do people say that I am?" Jesus pointedly redirects the question to his disciples, "But you, who do you say I am?" Responding for the group, Peter declares, "You are the Messiah (Greek, *christos*),"[12] in other words, God's "anointed one."[13] As the proclamation with which the Gospel opens indicates (1:1), the disciples' conclusion is correct: Jesus is the Messiah *(christos)*. But there's more to it than that; and so, after an odd admonition not to tell anyone about his identity as Messiah (8:30), Jesus then clarifies what his messianic identity entails. "Then he began to teach them that the Son of Man must *suffer many things*, and be rejected by the elders, the chief priests, and the scribes, and be killed, and after three days rise again" (8:31).

This is the first of three passion predictions, as scholars call them, which occur at 8:31, 9:31, and 10:33–34. This initial prediction is the only one to use the word "must" (in Greek, *dei*, also translated "it is necessary"), which is considered a theological passive, indicating the will of God, the implication being that what Jesus foresees for himself is a kind of divine necessity.[14] This theological passive, however, does not capture the fuller understanding of the will of God that is operative in Mark's Gospel as a whole. In this regard it is important to observe, first, that all three predictions include reference to the rising, or what we think of as the resurrection (hence my preference for designating them passion-resurrection predictions). These predictions warrant the theological conclusion not that God willed Jesus to suffer and die, as many Christians have been taught to think, but rather that God willed him to suffer, die, *and* rise. Second, it is equally important here to keep in mind Jesus' inaugural public proclamation, "The time is fulfilled, and the reign of God is at hand; repent, and believe in the good news" (1:14–15). This programmatic text summarizes the Markan understanding both of Jesus' mission and of the will of God; God wills to reign in this world and so raises up a Messiah and Son to walk the way of the Lord (1:2–11), proclaiming the dawn of that reign in mighty words and deeds. In Mark, then, everything that Jesus does—his preaching, teaching, exorcising, and feedings—is an expression of the will of God to reign.

But there is, as Jesus affirms early in the narrative, a "mystery" to the reign of God, a mystery given solely to disciples, not outsiders (4:11), and gradually revealed, to disciples and readers alike, in the course of the subsequent narrative. It is here, "on the way" to Jerusalem, that Jesus clarifies that mystery for his disciples by means of the three passion-resurrection predictions. The "mystery of the reign of God" is that the Messiah "must" suffer, die, and rise as Son of Man. That the disciples do not yet comprehend the mystery is made abundantly clear by Peter's response:[15] he dares to rebuke Jesus, thereby eliciting Jesus' stinging counter-rebuke, "Get behind me, Satan! You are thinking the things not of God but of humans" (4:33).[16]

After rebuking Peter, Jesus does what he will do after each of the three passion-resurrection predictions: he teaches about discipleship, which brings us to the verse pertinent to our interests. Calling the crowd with the disciples, Jesus declares, "If any want to become my followers, let them deny themselves and take up their cross and follow me" (8:34). It is the meaning of the references to self-denial and taking up the cross that are our primary concern. For centuries Christians have spiritualized both references, interpreting the first as a call to an ascetic way of life requiring denial of one's own will and desires, and the second as a call to bear patiently all sorts of personal hardship or suffering, including domestic abuse, as a "cross to bear" in imitation of Christ. Such interpretations are not only detrimental for women and other marginalized groups, but they are a misreading of Mark's Gospel.[17]

The original meaning of this verse must be determined in narrative context and by attention to the historical and cultural context in which the Markan author and audience lived, that is, a first-century Mediterranean world living under Roman imperial rule. Within that context proclamation of a reign other than that of Caesar put one on a collision course with Roman authorities, and in the case of Jesus' own historical ministry in Palestine, with the Jewish religious establishment that had negotiated an accommodation with the imperial regime in order to preserve its people's freedom to worship their God. Those proclaiming an alternative reign faced the real and present danger of persecution, including threat of execution, that would compel a torturous decision: to lose or to save one's own life. That the meaning of Mark 8:34, with its parallel references "deny themselves" and "take up their cross,"[18] must be interpreted in terms of such a context is indicated by the explanatory clause that immediately follows: "For those who want to save their life will lose it, and those who lose their life for my sake, and for the sake of the gospel, will save it" (8:35).

Given the context of persecution clearly implied by 8:35, no ancient audience would hear "take up your cross" as a call to embrace any and all hardship and suffering in following Jesus. Living in the aftermath of Nero's persecution of Christians, Mark and his community knew the politics of Roman rule—and of the cross—all too well, and so too the threat of persecution (Mk 13:9–13).[19] The cross was a brutal and utterly degrading form of punishment used by the Romans for those considered a threat to the imperial regime. Christians' allegiance to the rulership of God constituted such a challenge. They also knew that the suffering wrought by imperial persecution could be avoided by denying or renouncing one's allegiance to Jesus, as Peter does later in the narrative (14:66–72). Thus, in the original context, Jesus' reference to a cross would hardly be intended or construed metaphorically.

For the Markan audience the cross that Jesus took up, and the cross that disciples must be prepared to take up as well, "was not a difficult family situation, not a frustration of visions of personal fulfillment, a crushing debt or nagging in-law; it was the political, legally to be expected result of a moral clash with the powers ruling his society."[20] It was, literally, the apparatus on which Romans executed dissidents and troublemakers, brutally humiliating and degrading them in the public eye for the sake of deterrence.

Likewise, an ancient audience would not have construed "let them deny (or renounce) themselves" (8:34) as a call to give up one's own will and desires in an ascetic lifestyle, as Christians today are inclined to do. In ancient Mediterranean culture the kinship group, not the individual person, was the basic unit of society that determined selfhood and personal identity; to deny or renounce self was to renounce or deny one's kin. Such a decision was costly, for it meant the rejection of one's parents and the loss of the means of livelihood in which the kin group shared. It was also risky, because it threatened the foundation of the social-political-economic order of the empire. Thus, like daring to proclaim the reign or rulership of God, to deny oneself, that is, one's kin group, was to court persecution.[21]

This interpretation of "let them deny themselves" is confirmed by the only other occurrences in Mark of the verb "deny/renounce" (Greek *aparneomai* in 14:30, 31, 72). These refer to Peter's denial (14:54, 66–72), which frames the trial of Jesus before the high priest (14:55–65) in Mark. Here the evangelist's familiar framing technique serves to contrast Jesus' courageous confession of his identity as "the Messiah, the Son of the Blessed One" (14:61–62), a confession that costs him his life, with Peter's cowardly denial of Jesus to save his own. The poignancy of the scene is palpable for readers who recognize the links with earlier episodes, including Jesus' instruction in 8:34–35. Peter, like the other disciples, had made the costly choice to deny his kinship ties and his means of livelihood (nets) in order to follow Jesus (1:16–20). By doing so he had become a member of the new fictive kinship group with which Jesus identifies: "Here are my mother and my brothers. Whoever does the will of God is my brother and sister and mother" (3:35). Later, on the fateful "way" to Jerusalem, he heard Jesus' sobering admonition: a true disciple must be prepared to lose one's life "for my sake and for the sake of the gospel" (8:35). Finally, however, in what is his own "trial" of sorts in the courtyard, Peter proves unprepared to face the persecution that participation in his new fictive kinship entails. Whereas Jesus confesses to his accusers his kinship status as "son of the Blessed One" (14:61–62), thereby remaining steadfast in his commitment to "the will of God" to reign, in stark contrast Peter, by renouncing Jesus to save his own life, in effect renounces his new fictive kinship with those who seek to "do the will of God."

To summarize, then, the original meaning of Mark 8:34 is clarified by its narrative context—Jerusalem and Jesus' clash with the authorities looming on the horizon—and by its historical and cultural context—the first-century Mediterranean world under Roman rule. In these contexts Jesus' words for the crowd and disciples "on the way" to Jerusalem—"If any want to become my followers, let them deny themselves and take up their cross and follow me"—are less a call to discipleship than a frank and sobering forewarning for would-be disciples regarding the costs that they should expect to incur in following him on "the way of the Lord." In the words of a theologian attentive to the politics of the era, "To accept the cross as his destiny, to move toward it . . . when he could well have done otherwise, was Jesus' constantly reiterated free choice; and he warns his disciples lest their embarking on the same path be less conscious of its cost."[22] Indeed, critical study of Mark 8:34 indicates that the original meaning of this memorable and oft-quoted discipleship instruction is not an encouragement to or glorification of any and all suffering in human life or in Christian discipleship. Rather, it presumes a very specific context—persecution by the authorities—and pertains to a particular type of suffering that occurs in that context: the "apostolic suffering" that, due to the imperial "way" of the world, includes various types of rejection, ridicule, ostracism, humiliation, and punitive tactics, some deadly, that the "supposed authorities" (10:42), threatened by the advocates of God's reign, will inflict upon them.[23]

Suffering in the Gospel of Mark

Having clarified the original meaning of the single Markan text that has, arguably, done more to shape Christian attitudes toward suffering, for good and for ill, than any other, we turn now to the Gospel as a whole to consider what more it offers for our theological reflection. Happily for us, Mark's Gospel proves to be a rich source of material on the subject, for, as even the casual reader soon recognizes, suffering is writ large across the length of Mark's narrative. Parents with sick, dying, or possessed children; women and men afflicted by physical or spiritual maladies; crowds hungry for teaching and for food—these are the characters who inhabit the Markan stage throughout the first ten chapters and assume center-stage at its climax, the physical, emotional, and spiritual torment of a man dogged by religious authorities, then tortured, ridiculed, humiliated unto death, his followers left to anoint, bury, and grieve him.

The sheer volume of material relevant to our interest and the constraints of space require that we focus our attention on a few carefully chosen passages within the narrative. Somewhat surprisingly, there are only three occurrences of the Greek word for "suffering" (*paschein*, "to suffer, endure, undergo") in Mark, always in the construction "to *suffer* many things," one referencing a hemorrhaging woman (5:26), and two, the passion of the Son of Man (8:31; 9:12). These three uses of the word advise us to focus our attention on the experience and responses of two sufferers, the hemorrhaging woman and Jesus, whose stories have much to teach in the way of wisdom about the experience of suffering, our own and that of others, including appropriate responses to it. That particular choice of material will permit us to examine both a representative case of common human suffering (that of the hemorrhaging woman) and the Markan account of the messianic suffering of Jesus, which, as Jesus' admonition in 8:34–35 implies, provides the pattern for the apostolic suffering of his disciples.

The Hemorrhaging Woman: Model of Self-Care

Throughout the first ten chapters of Mark's Gospel, Jesus' proclamation of the reign of God (1:14–15) is accompanied by mighty
deeds in which Jesus repeatedly responds to human suffering:
healing the sick and disabled, freeing people from demons, feeding
the hungry despite scarce resources, stilling the storm that threatens safety. Thus, in Mark, God's will to reign brings relief from
the myriad forms of privation that cause suffering and threaten
personal and communal wholeness and well-being *(shalom)*. In
addition, he authorizes and sends out his disciples to do the same,
and they do so successfully (6:7–13). Thus, for Mark, healings, exorcisms, and feedings are the blessings of God's in-breaking reign.

Among Mark's many episodes about suppliants who experience
the powerful blessings of that reign, the story of the hemorrhaging
woman is one of the most remarkable and for the purposes of our
reflection, one of the most valuable. The extraordinary interaction
between Jesus and the woman that occurs in this episode permits
us to witness two responses to the woman's suffering, her own
and that of Jesus.

Feminist biblical scholarship has drawn attention to the parallel
between the hemorrhaging woman and Jesus. The striking verbal
links between their stories, which are obscured in most English
translations but readily recognizable in the Greek, include the
words for "suffering" *(paschein,* 5:26; 8:31; 9:12), "affliction"
(mastigos, 5:29,34; 10:34), "blood" *(haimatos,* 5:25; 14:24), and
telling "the truth" *(alētheia,* 5:33; 12:32). Based on these links
the woman's story has been read as prefiguring Jesus' passion.[24]
These links also serve to remind us that, although there is in Mark
a significant distinction between the messianic sufferings of Jesus,
upon which the apostolic suffering of disciples is patterned, and
the more common human suffering of the suppliants who come to
him, these types of suffering are not unrelated. Both are composed
of the same basic elements: undergoing or enduring, blood and the
threat of death, affliction.

Not unlike the earlier description of the suffering that Jesus will
experience (10:32–34), the opening verses of the episode present

the woman's plight in graphic detail: "Now there was a woman who had had a *flow of blood* for twelve years. She had *suffered* much under many physicians, and had spent all that she had; and she was no better, but rather grew worse" (5:25–26). It is not entirely clear what her physical malady is. Most commentators presume chronic abnormal vaginal or uterine bleeding.[25] Apparently at one time she had been a woman of some means, able to afford the services of physicians, but their ineffectual treatment simply left her impoverished ("she had spent all that she had") and debilitated ("she was no better but only grew worse").[26] Thus, her suffering entails multiple forms of privation: loss of blood that would diminish her physically; loss of economic resources; loss of twelve years of her life; and apparently loss of relationality (the lack of reference to anyone accompanying her).

To this list of her sufferings some commentators (and preachers) insist on adding, even emphasizing, social ostracism caused by her unclean status. Citing ancient Israel's purity code (Lv 15:19–33), they claim that her suffering is compounded by a religious community that shuns her, making her an outcast. Nothing in this pericope, however, draws attention to the woman's unclean and outcast status. Indeed, the crowd shows no surprise or concern that this woman is in their midst despite the twelve-year malady that has taken her to physicians. Given that elsewhere Mark quite explicitly engages purity issues (7:1–23; 1:40–44), the absence of any such reference in this pericope is, I suggest, telling and should be respected for the purposes of interpretation.[27] There is no need to account for her apparent isolation by reference to Israel's purity code; for there are in fact alternative explanations. For example, in the ancient context, as today, an intractable chronic illness is sufficient cause of a sufferer's isolation.[28] In the absence of a clear textual basis for the claim that "the many things she suffered" included shunning by her Jewish community and since "it is unclear to what extent Galilean peasant women at the time of Jesus observed the laws of menstrual purity,"[29] commentators should be wary of introducing this unnecessary assumption into our interpretation of this woman's story; the text itself explicitly details what her sufferings included: misplaced trust in physicians, lack of relief, economic disaster, and apparently lack of anyone to advocate for her.

Significant for our purposes is the woman's attitude toward and response to her suffering. Apparently throughout her twelve-year affliction she has sought the assistance of multiple physicians, suggesting a tenacious desire and determination to be well. More remarkably, despite the fact that her recourse to physicians during her long ordeal proved fruitless, she is neither resigned to her condition nor is her desire to be well diminished. Rather, her desire is quickened upon hearing about Jesus (5:27), and so she acts. Working her way through the jostling crowd, she approaches Jesus from behind, reaches out to touch his garment, saying, "If I but touch his clothes, I will be made well" (5:27–28), and at last she is healed of the blood-flow (5:29).[30] As numerous commentators note, one of the most extraordinary features of the hemorrhaging woman's story is that her healing occurs at her own initiative. Unresigned to her suffering, taking matters into her own hands, she does what is in her power to do: she reaches out, yet again, in hope of relief, to one whom she believes can heal her. The decision to do so is entirely her own. Moreover, she neither requests the healing nor seeks anyone's permission to do what she does. She simply seizes the opportunity that Jesus' presence affords her, and her healing instantly occurs, at her own initiative, without even the compliance of Jesus. Thus, by means of her bold and determined outreach for herself, she accesses the incomparable power available in and through Jesus. In this she is a model of self-care.

She is not the only character who affords a model response to suffering for our reflection, however. Once Jesus feels the power go out of him, he seeks to identify the person who accessed that power and for what purpose. In response to Jesus' question—"Who touched my clothes?"—the woman, "knowing what had happened to her, came in fear and trembling, fell down before him, and told him the whole truth" (5:33). Based on her posture, her "fear and trembling," and the reference to telling the truth, some commentators construe her action as a confession of wrongdoing that is warranted by her bold action in daring to touch this man. This, however, is a misreading that overlooks the meaning of this posture and of "fear and trembling" in Mark's larger narrative. In the biblical tradition, including elsewhere in Mark, falling to the ground in "fear and trembling" is the appropriate expression of awe in the presence of the holy. Thus, the woman's response to Jesus' query indicates her spiritual awareness that what has happened to her is "of the holy God."[31] Similarly, her telling "the whole truth" need not be construed as a confession of wrongdoing on her part. Rather, Jesus' question affords her opportunity to tell him her whole story—of long-suffering, visits to physicians, economic ruin, and the hope that news of him inspired.

Jesus' response to the woman is significant for our interests. First, Jesus' question, "Who touched my clothes?" affords an opportunity for this woman to find the voice of which suffering often robs persons who suffer.[32] Second, he neither scolds her for her refusal to resign herself to suffering nor chides her bold initiative on her own behalf. No "How dare you do this, Woman?! Do you not know that this is your cross to bear?" but instead, "Daughter, your faith has made you well." Jesus' words to her deserve our attention. Most important, by addressing the woman as daughter, Jesus ends the social isolation that the woman has long suffered.[33] In addition, rather than claiming credit for the healing—after all, the power that healed her resided in Jesus—he attributes it to her, citing the woman's own faith as its cause. In Mark, "faith" is not intellectual assent to specific theological propositions. It is a relational term that combines trust and confidence, more precisely, trust in the good will of and confidence in the power of God and/or Jesus. Thus, the faith that Jesus lauds here is the woman's resolute trust that God wills the good for her, in this case, the restoration of her health and wholeness, and her confidence that the power present in Jesus, about which she, like the swarming crowd, had heard, can provide it ("If I but touch his clothes, I will be made well."). Last, Jesus' affirmation of the woman's faith also illumines the dynamic at work in the healing, which is unique in that it occurs apart from the will and intention of Jesus. Instead, power goes out of him at the woman's touch. Touch alone, however, is not what affects the release of power, for we may presume that others in the swarming crowd are touching Jesus. As Jesus' words indicate, it is the faith of the woman that impels her touch and facilitates the healing. Her faith, that is, her trust and confidence in him, activates and releases the power in Jesus. Thus, commentator Mary Rose D'Angelo rightly identifies in the story "a Christology of shared spiritual power, one in which Jesus' power is active through the participation of others."[34]

Mark's story of this long-suffering woman is instructive for our ongoing reflection on appropriate attitudes toward and responses to suffering. Indeed, both the woman and Jesus model for us what we might term "gospel" attitudes and responses to suffering, the woman to her own, and Jesus to that of another. Despite a twelve-year affliction from which she has found no relief but has only "grown worse," the woman remains determined to be well. Long-suffering though she may be, she is not resigned to suffering as her lot in life; rather, she wants more for herself, trusts that it can and should be, and takes care to get it when news of Jesus' power affords reason for hope. By her own courageous initiative, she reaches out to Jesus, the one whom she believes can help her, and secures the wholeness of which she has been deprived. Significantly, despite the fact that the woman accessed his power without his consent, and in so doing violated Mediterranean cultural norms for submissive female behavior, Jesus does not reprimand her for her bold initiative. Instead, he listens to her story, by which she finds her voice. And then he affirms her faith-filled initiative on behalf of her own well-being, "Daughter, your faith has made you well." This long-suffering woman refused to accept this suffering as her lot in life; and Jesus, in effect, affirms her determined stance to be free of it. Like the many other stories of suffering suppliants in this and other Gospels, there is here no counsel to "grin and bear it," to "offer it up, dear," or "take up your cross, woman," but rather praise, "Daughter, your faith has made you well." For both this woman and for Jesus, this long ordeal was not her "cross to bear." It was, rather, an occasion for the reign of God to draw near.

Jesus in Gethsemane: Prayer in Crisis

Throughout the first ten chapters of Mark, Jesus repeatedly responds to the suffering of others as he goes about his mission on behalf of the in-breaking reign of God. Fidelity to that messianic mission, however, eventually brings an especially brutal suffering upon him. Two episodes of Mark's passion narrative invite us to reflect further on Jesus' response to suffering, in this case, his own. In doing so, we ought to recall that while "on the way" to Jerusalem with his disciples, three times Jesus speaks quite matter of factly of his destiny—his suffering, dying, and rising as Son of Man—doing so without any sign of distress (8:31; 9:31; 10:33–34).[35] When Jesus arrives in Jerusalem, however, his demeanor is strikingly different. The startling change is first evident in Gethsemane where, with "the hour" now at hand, "he threw himself on the ground and prayed that, if it were possible, the hour might pass from him" (14:35). The prospect of the suffering, dying, and rising now becomes for Jesus a grave crisis. The nature of that crisis is clarified by Jesus' final instruction to his disciples: "Keep awake and pray that you may not come into the time of trial (Greek *peirasmos*); the spirit is willing but the flesh is weak" (14:38). Jesus experiences the arrival of the "hour" for the drinking of the "cup" as a *peirasmos*, which in Greek bears the threefold meaning test, trial, and temptation; and he does so, by his own admission, because "the spirit is willing but the flesh is weak."[36] Just as earlier he forewarns would-be disciples about the persecution that would likely be their lot as his followers, here Jesus admonishes the disciples to watch and to pray in order that they may not undergo a *peirasmos* as he does.[37]

In marked contrast to the sleeping disciples, Jesus deals with this crisis of the flesh through prayer. It begins with intimate address ("*Abba*, Father"), followed by an expression of faith, "all things are possible for you," that acknowledges the freedom and power of God to accomplish whatever God wills. Then, in the context of the relationship of trust implied by the intimate address, Jesus voices a stunningly forthright request: "*Take* this cup [in other words, this measure of suffering] *away* from me" (14:36). In his conversation with James and John on the way to Jerusalem, Jesus had spoken, without flinching, of "the cup that I drink" (10:38).[38] And in the Passover meal that immediately preceded the withdrawal to Gethsemane, with no sign of distress Jesus had declared over the shared cup, "This is my blood of the covenant, which is poured out for many" (14:24). But in Gethsemane Jesus' willing spirit is tried, tested, and tempted as his flesh, in its vulnerability to pain and death, and so to fear, recoils at the prospect of actually drinking the cup. Significantly, although the desire of Jesus' flesh is at odds with what he knows to be the will of God, he does not hesitate to express that contrary desire to the Father. Then, in the midst of his intense distress Jesus manages to add, "Yet not what I will but what you will" (14:36). Lest we hastily conclude that the words "not what I will but what you will" signal the end of his struggle, it is important to note that after getting up and finding the disciples asleep, "he again went away and prayed, saying the same words" (14:39). Jesus persists in prayer, voicing his petition a second, and even seemingly, a third time (14:37, 39, 41), while the disciples sleep. Braced by the power of prayer, Jesus resolves to "drink the cup": "The hour has come; the Son of Man is betrayed into the hands of sinners. Get up, let us be going. See, my betrayer is at hand" (14:41–42).

The Markan account of Jesus' experience in Gethsemane affords ample material for our reflection on suffering and Christian discipleship. Perhaps most important, it is clear that despite his conviction that his suffering, dying, and rising "must" happen in accord with God's will to reign, Jesus struggles, long and hard, in Gethsemane. That struggle confirms that Jesus is no masochist, wishing to suffer. Rather, in the fullness of his humanity ("the flesh"), Jesus desires to live and is deeply distressed at the prospect of the cross. He neither welcomes the torture that a Roman cross entailed nor is he blindly obedient and submissive to Abba's will, for in the midst of his struggle with his messianic fate he forthrightly expresses himself, including his desire that this "cup" be removed, in effect, that Abba change the script. In this, Jesus models for disciples the courage to pray in times of trial *(peirasmos)*, of adversity, which, as his admonition for would-be disciples apprises us (8:34–35), will likely come for those who follow him. Finally, it is important to recognize that the Markan Jesus in Gethsemane is also not a passive and resigned victim. Rather, by means of his steadfast and prayerful struggle with Abba's will, at the end of the scene Jesus resolves to go forward, "Get up, let us be going. See, my betrayer is at hand" (14:42); and he will do so alone when all the disciples, abandoning him, flee to save themselves (15:50).

Jesus on Golgotha: Faithful Lamentation

On Golgotha, it is clear that Jesus' steadfast resolve to entrust himself to Abba's will neither lessens his pain of the flesh nor exempts him from the torment of the crucified. Mark's grim crucifixion scene emphasizes that Jesus dies terribly alone. The disciples having fled at his arrest, Jesus hangs on the cross in a kind of solitary confinement with no one near but his executioners and enemies, who ridicule, taunt, and make sport of his powerlessness (15:29–32). His social isolation apparently complete, he makes no complaint to taunting bystanders and executioners. Jesus does not, however, die quietly, docilely, and submissively. Rather, with the opening words of Psalm 22, he lifts his voice to the heavens in a loud cry: "My God, my God, why have you forsaken me?" (15:34). In the Markan account these are the only words, and the last words, of Jesus on the cross. Because of their immense significance for our reflection on the subject of suffering, it is important that we interpret them rightly.

For many Christians, Jesus' cry on the cross sounds like a cry of despair that seems inappropriate, even inconceivable, on the lips of the Son of God. To render it less theologically problematic, they claim that Mark intends us to recognize that Jesus prayed the entirety of Psalm 22, which concludes with praise and confidence in deliverance by God (23–32). Such an interpretation softens the desperation and protest with which these interpreters are uncomfortable, but it does so at the expense of the Markan Gospel and its narrative logic. The Markan Jesus' last words are a cry, not of despair, but of unmitigated abandonment, a cry from the depths of the "mystery" into which he is "baptized" (10:38).

Thus, on the cross Jesus does what his people had done for generations: he cries out to God in lamentation, using the words of a psalm of lament (Ps 22:1). It was by means of the many laments in the psalter of Israel that the suffering righteous brought to their covenant-God their experiences of negativity, of pain and distress, of injustice, and of innocent suffering, hence their alternate designation "psalms of the suffering righteous."[39] That Jesus in Mark is a suffering righteous one, one in right relationship with God, is clear. His walk on "the way of the Lord" began with his baptism in the Spirit, when the heavenly voice claimed him, "You are my Son, the Beloved; with you I am well pleased" (Mk 1:11). Subsequently, this Son lived up to those words, proclaiming the in-breaking of God's reign among his people, healing the sick, freeing the possessed from the grip of evil, feeding hungry crowds, even embracing the "mystery" (4:11) that the coming of God's reign would require far more than glorious mighty deeds (8:31; 9:31; 10:33–34). In Gethsemane, this Son, experiencing that "the spirit is willing but the flesh weak," struggled mightily and prayerfully through his crisis of the flesh. In short, the Markan Jesus comes to the cross as the trusting obedient Son, God's righteous one, only to experience the atrocious absence of Abba.[40]

In narrative context the absence of Abba on Golgotha threatens to strip Jesus of the one thing not yet taken from him, the conviction that this terrible happening is not as absurd as the taunts of bystanders suggest, that in truth it has meaning. The Son has come to the cross believing the mystery into which he is "baptized" to be the will of God (8:31; 10:38);[41] and so, why Abba's absence? The Markan Jesus' last words are, then, not a last-minute cry for divine intervention, for in Gethsemane he had entrusted himself to Abba's will. They are, rather, a cry for that divine presence upon which the meaning of this terrible event depends, a cry for meaning and for solidarity in the "mystery" into which he is here plunged.

Jesus' last words may also be read as a cry of protest, although Christians are often uncomfortable, even troubled, by this suggestion. Such a Jesus, Son of God, is difficult for many to assimilate. But critical study of the faith and prayer practices of ancient Israel, including the lament traditions, provides a solid foundation for this interpretation. As Old Testament scholar Walter Brueggemann has observed, the laments in Israel's prayer book are bold speech, the kind of bold speech that occurs in the deep and durable relationship called covenant, which began with God's declaration of election, "you will be my people and I will be your God" (Ex 6:7; Lv 26:12). In the context of Israel's covenant life with Yahweh, the laments, including Psalm 22, are a complaint that insists: "Things are not right here! They can be changed. God, you make it right!"[42] Similarly, Jesus' special relationship with God, his sonship, began with a declaration of election from the heavens, "You are my beloved Son. On you my favor rests" (1:11). In the context of that divinely initiated relationship, Jesus' lament is the beloved Son's bold cry of protest that this terrible aloneness is not right, not the way it should be. It is, as it was for his fellow Jews, speech that bespeaks a bold faith that dares to cry for justice to the heavens, source of all justice.[43]

In Mark's Golgotha account, there is no reply to this protesting cry for presence and for meaning. As at Gethsemane, the heavenly voice remains deadly silent.[44] At the denouement of the Markan drama, however, readers learn that Abba did not, ultimately, abandon his Son, for there is good news, delivered by a heavenly messenger at the tomb: "You are looking for Jesus of Nazareth, who was crucified. He has been raised" (16:6). God's unfathomable will—that the Son of Man "must" suffer, die, and rise—is accomplished. The Crucified One, now raised, is once again "on the way" to Galilee, where the disciples, even Peter, will see him (16:7).

The Markan presentation of the suffering and death of Jesus is, I believe, an especially precious resource for Christian reflection on suffering, one that deserves far more comment than space allows here. Above all and most important, Mark's grim account of Jesus' crucifixion and death, with Jesus' lamenting protest at its climax, should disabuse us of any tendency to glorify the cross. On Golgotha Jesus the Messiah *(christos)* is plunged into the "mystery of the reign of God" and from its dark depths utters a last desperate cry. And that cry in itself is instructive for us; for Jesus' lamentation from the depths of suffering authorizes disciples to pray as he did, with bold speech. Like our Jewish forebears, we ought, as individuals and in liturgical assemblies, dare to raise our voices to the heavens in complaint and protest in the face of the unspeakable suffering and calamity, the grave injustices that people experience in our times.

Conclusion

This essay has sought to identify the potential Markan contribution to theological reflection on suffering that is urgently needed in our contemporary context. Due to the constraints of space, our examination of Markan material has been selective, and so it hardly does justice to the rich resources that the earliest of our canonical Gospels affords for our reflection. Based on our exploration of these select passages, by way of conclusion I wish to make a few general observations regarding the Markan understanding of suffering and discipleship.

First, Mark's Gospel distinguishes between general human suffering, such as that of the hemorrhaging woman, and the messianic suffering of Jesus on which the apostolic suffering of Christian disciples is patterned. It is the former that is addressed and alleviated by Jesus and his disciples, and the latter that disciples must be prepared to accept and resolutely endure, as Jesus did. The distinction between the two types of suffering does not mean, however, that they are unrelated. In Mark, Jesus' ministry to those who suffer is part of his mission on behalf of the reign of God, and that mission provokes the hostility of the authorities, who eventually condemn him to the cross. As Jesus' admonition to would-be disciples makes clear, those who carry on his mission, proclaiming the reign of God to all the nations (13:10) and working to relieve and alleviate the suffering of others, can expect that their allegiance to God's reign will bring them their own "cup" to drink.

Second, Mark's Gospel offers no explanation of human suffering. Suffering simply bulks large in the story, as it does in reality; rather than explain it, Mark narrates the promise of its relief with God's in-breaking reign. Thus, Mark does not claim that God wills suffering, that suffering is good for us, or that suffering alone saves, as some Christians have come to believe. The Markan narrative does, however, offer an explanation of the particular suffering of Jesus. It is one part of "the mystery of the reign of God" that, by the inscrutable will of God, "must" occur. But as the formulation of Jesus' predictions of his fate makes clear, God does not will the Son of Man to suffer and die; God wills him to suffer, die, and rise. Thus, Mark provides no basis for glorification or valorization of suffering, including the suffering of Jesus on the cross.

Third, the praxis of Jesus the Messiah is now the praxis of the discipleship community: proclamation of the reign of God in word and deed. In following the Crucified-One-Now-Raised back to Galilee (16:7), disciples do what "must" be done in the time that stretches from resurrection to *parousia* (the coming of the reign in its full power). "The gospel must be preached to all nations" (13:10), and human suffering, in its myriad forms, must be relieved—by healing, forgiving, teaching, confronting evil, feeding the hungry. Along "the way," disciples must be prepared to "take up the cross" when those whose self-serving authority opposes God's rule inflict various forms of suffering upon them.

Finally, in its startlingly grim presentation of Jesus' cry from the depths and in its interpretation of Jesus' suffering in terms of "the mystery of the reign of God," Mark's Gospel offers us perhaps the truly seminal wisdom that can sustain us "on the way." It has to do with mystery and with presence, neither of which explains or justifies suffering, but both of which may point a way through it. On Golgotha Jesus cried to the heavens from the depths of "the mystery." It was a cry for presence, for the felt presence of relationship in the midst of suffering. And here the comments of two theologians come to mind, both of which, I suggest, illumine Jesus' cry from the cross. In her comments on Psalm 130, Wendy Farley observes:

> If suffering were to be made intelligible, that might help us retain . . . an experience of meaningfulness in the face of our own and others' suffering. But suffering does not require explanation so much as redemption. There simply do not exist words or ideas or concepts that can undo the savagery of the suffering to which we are subject as creatures with bodies and loved ones. But what concepts cannot do, relationships can.[45]

And finally, in an essay on suffering in the Gospel of Mark, it seems eminently fitting that "mystery" have the last word. Walter Kasper writes: "No one has experienced humanity to the full unless he or she has experienced its finiteness and suffering. But then experience becomes a way of leading into an open immensity, into a mystery that is ever greater and never to be completely plumbed."[46]

Notes

1. The work of healthcare professionals, who address pain and suffering on a daily basis, affords valuable insights into this experience. See, for example, Eric Cassell, *The Nature of Suffering and the Goals of Medicine* (New York: Oxford University Press, 1991); Margaret Mohrmann and Mark J. Hanson, eds., *Pain Seeking Understanding: Suffering, Medicine, and Faith* (Cleveland: Pilgrim Press, 1999); Margaret Mohrmann, *Medicine as Ministry: Reflections on Suffering, Ethics, and Hope* (Cleveland: Pilgrim Press, 1995). For a theologian's reflections on suffering and medicine, see Stanley Hauerwas, *Suffering Presence: Theological Reflections on Medicine, the Mentally Handicapped, and the Church* (Notre Dame, IN: University of Notre Dame Press, 1986); and Joel Shuman and Brian Volck, M.D., *Reclaiming the Body: Christians and the Faithful Use of Modern Medicine* (Grand Rapids, MI: Brazos Press, 2006). The work of medical anthropologists and medical sociologists also affords perspectives useful for theological reflection; see Arthur Kleinman, M.D., *The Illness Narratives: Suffering, Healing, and the Human Condition* (New York: Basic Books, 1988); and Arthur W. Frank, *The Wounded Storyteller: Body, Illness, and Ethics* (Chicago: University of Chicago Press, 1995).

2. See Benjamin R. Barber, *Consumed: How Markets Corrupt Children, Infantilize Adults, and Swallow Citizens Whole* (New York: W. W. Norton, 2007); and Chris Hedges, *Empire of Illusion: The End of Literacy and the Triumph of Spectacle* (New York: Nation Books, 2009).

3. For feminist theology, see Catherine Mowry LaCugna, ed., *Freeing Theology: The Essentials of Theology in Feminist Perspective* (San Francisco: Harper San Francisco, 1993); Rosemary Radford Ruether, *Sexism and God-Talk: Toward a Feminist Theology* (Boston: Beacon Press, 1993); Elizabeth A. Johnson, *She Who Is: The Mystery of God in Feminist Theological Discourse* (New York: Crossroad, 1994); Rita Nakashima

Brock, Claudia Camp, and Serene Jones, eds., *Setting the Table: Women in Theological Conversation* (St. Louis: Chalice Press, 1995); Susan Abraham and Elena Procario-Foley, eds., *Frontiers in Catholic Feminist Theology: Shoulder to Shoulder* (Minneapolis: Fortress Press, 2009). For an excellent introduction, see Anne M. Clifford, *Introducing Feminist Theology* (Maryknoll, NY: Orbis Books, 2001). Christian women of color, who identify themselves as womanists (rather than feminists) in recognition of the fact that their own struggles as women are compounded by their racial and class identities, also theologize out of a critical consciousness that is sharpened by the multiplicative oppression that women of color experience. See Stephanie Y. Mitchem, *Introducing Womanist Theology* (Maryknoll, NY: Orbis Books, 2002); Delores S. Williams, *Sisters in the Wilderness: The Challenge of Womanist God-Talk* (Maryknoll, NY: Orbis Books, 2004); Karen Baker-Fletcher, *Dancing with God: The Trinity from a Womanist Perspective* (St. Louis: Chalice Press, 2006); Monica Coleman, *Making a Way Out of No Way: A Womanist Theology* (Minneapolis: Fortress Press, 2008); Diana Hayes, *Standing in the Shoes My Mother Made: A Womanist Theology* (Minneapolis: Fortress Press, 2011). From Hispanic and Latina women, see Ada María Isasi-Díaz, *En la Lucha: In the Struggle: Elaborating a Mujerista Theology* (Minneapolis: Fortress Press, 1993); María Pilar Aquino, *Our Cry for Life: Feminist Theology from Latin America* (Maryknoll, NY: Orbis Books, 1993); Elsa Tamez, ed., *Through Her Eyes: Women's Theology from Latin America* (Eugene, OR: Wipf and Stock, 2006). From the larger two-thirds world, see Virginia Fabella and Mercy Amba Oduyoye, eds., *With Passion and Compassion: Third World Women Doing Theology* (Maryknoll, NY: Orbis Books, 1988).

4. On the problem of gendered God-language, see Elizabeth Johnson, "The Incomprehensibility of God and the Image of God Male and Female," *Theological Studies* 45 (1984): 441–65; Catherine LaCugna, "The Baptismal Formula, Feminist Objections, and Trinitarian Theology," *Journal of Ecumenical Studies* 26 (1989): 235 50; and Gail Ramshaw, *God Beyond Gender: Feminist Christian God-Language* (Minneapolis: Fortress Press, 1995). On the biblical roots of our God-language, see Sandra Schneiders, *Women and the Word: The Gender of God in the New Testament and the Spirituality of Women,* Madeleva Lecture in Spirituality #1986 (New York: Paulist Press, 1986).

5. See the classic critique by Joanne Carlson Brown and Rebecca Parker, "For God So Loved the World?" in *Christianity, Patriarchy, and Abuse: A Feminist Critique*, ed. Joanne Carlson Brown and Carole R.

Bohn, 1–30 (New York: Pilgrim, 1989). Numerous feminist and womanist theologians have articulated such a critique and/or set forth alternative theological constructions of suffering, servanthood, and sacrifice. See, for example, Delores S. Williams, "Black Women's Surrogacy Experience Challenges Christian Notions of Redemption," in *After Patriarchy*, ed. Paula Cooney et al., 1–14 (Maryknoll, NY: Orbis Books, 1991); Emilie Townes, ed., *A Troubling in My Soul: Womanist Perspectives on Evil and Suffering* (Maryknoll, NY: Orbis Books, 1996); Jacquelyn Grant, "The Sin of Servanthood and the Deliverance of Discipleship," in Townes, *A Troubling in My Soul*, 199–218; Kathleen Darby Ray, *Deceiving the Devil: Atonement, Abuse, and Ransom* (Cleveland: Pilgrim, 2001); Cynthia Crysdale, *Embracing Travail: Retrieving the Cross Today* (New York: Continuum, 1999); Sharon Thornton, *Broken Yet Beloved: A Pastoral Theology of the Cross* (St. Louis: Chalice Press, 2002); Barbara Reid, *Taking Up the Cross: New Testament Interpretations Through Latina and Feminist Eyes* (Minneapolis: Fortress Press, 2007); and Erin Lothes Biviano, *The Paradox of Christian Sacrifice: The Loss of Self, the Gift of Self* (New York: Crossroad, 2007), which includes a chapter entitled "The Feminist Critique of a Distorted Ideal of Sacrifice" (71–118).

   6. Feminist scholars are not alone in recognizing the pernicious effects of some theologies of suffering and the cross. The numerous books on the cross and on atonement that have appeared in recent years evidence a growing recognition among theologians, Catholic and Protestant alike, of the need to articulate afresh the profound mysteries and truths by which Christians seek to live in light of cross and empty tomb. See, for example, Joel B. Green and Mark D. Baker, *Recovering the Scandal of the Cross: Atonement in New Testament and Contemporary Contexts* (Downers Grove, IL: IVP Academic, 2000); Stephen Finlan, *Problems with Atonement: The Origins of, and Controversy About, the Atonement Doctrine* (Collegeville, MN: Liturgical Press, 2005); and idem, *Options on Atonement in Christian Thought* (Collegeville, MN: Liturgical Press, 2007); S. Mark Heim, *Saved from Sacrifice: A Theology of the Cross* (Grand Rapids, MI: Eerdmans, 2006); Mart Trelstead, ed., *Cross Examinations: Readings on the Meaning of the Cross Today* (Minneapolis: Fortress Press, 2006); Robert J. Daly, *Sacrifice Unveiled: The True Meaning of Christian Sacrifice* (New York: T & T Clark, 2009); and James H. Cone, *The Cross and the Lynching Tree* (Maryknoll, NY: Orbis Books, 2011).

   7. Brown and Parker, "For God So Loved the World?" 26.

   8. See Joanne Carlson Brown and Carole R. Bohn, eds., *Christianity, Patriarchy, and Abuse: A Feminist Critique* (New York: Pilgrim, 1989);

Carol J. Adams and Marie M. Fortune, eds., *Violence Against Women and Children: A Christian Theological Sourcebook* (New York: Continuum, 1995); Christine E. Gudorf, *Victimization: Examining Christian Complicity* (Philadelphia: Trinity Press International, 1992); and Rita Nakashima Brock and Rebecca Ann Parker, *Proverbs of Ashes: Violence, Redemptive Suffering, and the Search for What Saves Us* (Boston: Beacon Press, 2001).

9. Green and Baker, *Recovering the Scandal*, 174. Here the authors are paraphrasing the feminist critique of Darby Kathleen Ray in her *Deceiving the Devil*.

10. There is a growing literature documenting women's experience of oppression around the world. See Nicholas D. Kristof and Sheryl WuDunn, *Half the Sky: Turning Oppression into Opportunity for Women Worldwide* (New York: Alfred A. Knopf, 2009); and Lisa Shannon, *A Thousand Sisters: My Journey into the Worst Place on Earth to Be a Woman* (Berkeley, CA : Seal Press, 2011).

11. This central section of Mark's Gospel is structured around three predictions or portents of Jesus' fate (8:31; 9:31; 10:33–34), each of which is followed by evidence of the disciples' incomprehension of that fate (8:32–33; 9:33–37; 10:35–37), which in turn occasions a lesson from Jesus about discipleship (8:34–38; 9:35–37; 10:38–45).

12. Unless otherwise indicated, all translations of the Greek text are from the New Revised Standard Version (NRSV). My occasional modifications are indicated by italics.

13. The text does not identify what has prompted Peter's conclusion. Based on narrative developments, however, readers may assume that Peter's answer is the result of reflection on what the disciples have witnessed in walking the "way" to this point: proclamation of the reign of God, powerful healings and exorcisms, and wilderness feedings reminiscent of the first exodus and of the messianic banquet that Isaiah had envisioned. All of these presage the messianic age.

14. Although Jesus does not speak in the first person in the three predictions, it is evident that he uses the phrase Son of Man self-referentially to describe his own destiny. Peter apparently thinks Jesus is talking about himself here, but as his subsequent rebuke of Jesus makes clear, he does not yet comprehend or accept what Jesus foresees ahead.

15. In the first-century Judaisms of which Jesus was a part, there were various conceptions about what the messiah would be like, but none involved a messiah who would suffer, die, and rise on a Roman cross. Rather, the hoped-for messiah, whether priest, prophet, or kingly figure

like David of old, would be a glorious and powerful figure. Hence, although the disciples have concluded, based on Jesus' powerfully life-giving words and deeds, that he is the messiah who inaugurates God's reign, they are unprepared to grasp the mystery of a divine rule that "must" be established by way of the suffering, dying, and rising of God's *christo*s.

16. Jesus' words are reminiscent of Isaiah 55:8–9: "For my thoughts are not your thoughts, nor are your ways my ways, says the Lord. For as the heavens are higher than the earth, so are my ways higher than your ways and my thoughts than your thoughts." The disciples' incomprehension of what "must" happen is evident in the second and third passion-resurrection predictions as well. After the second (9:31) Jesus discovers the disciples arguing about "who is the greatest" among them (9:33–34). After the third (10:33–34) James and John make the impertinent request, "Grant us to sit, one at your right hand and one at your left, in your glory" (10:37). In other words, they want the seats of power and prestige on each side of Jesus at the messianic banquet in the reign/kingdom of God. In response, Jesus questions them regarding their readiness for the baptism with which he will be baptized and for the cup that he will drink (10:38). Based on Mark's narrative logic, both the "baptism with which I am baptized" and "the cup that I drink" are metaphors for his (and later, their) baptism into and participation in the "mystery of the reign of God," that is, the suffering, dying, and rising to which Jesus refers in the three passion-resurrection predictions.

17. In her feminist reading of this pericope, Joanna Dewey rightly observes: "If read out of context and with modern Western understandings, the invitation can be understood as a glorification of suffering and an encouragement to become a victim: one is to deny oneself, sacrifice oneself, wipe out any sense of self, and to embrace the cross, that is, suffering in general. Many a woman has failed to develop her own identity and strengths and has embraced or endured suffering that could be alleviated because she has come to believe that such a way of life is pleasing to God and an imitation of Christ." See "'Let Them Renounce Themselves and Take Up Their Cross': A Feminist Reading of Mark 8:34 in Mark's Social and Narrative World," in *A Feminist Companion to Mark*, ed. Amy-Jill Levine, 23–36 (Sheffield, UK: Sheffield Academic Press, 2001), 23.

18. The chiastic structure of 8:34 offers clues for interpretation here. That structure is diagrammed: A If any want to follow me; B let them renounce themselves; B´ and take up their cross ; A´ and follow me. In chiastic structure the parallelism between the outer brackets, A and A´

(both referring to following Jesus), suggests that the meaning of B and B´ are similar to each other. In this case it is the explanatory clause that immediately follows in 8:35 that clarifies what the similarity of B and B´ is: both presume the threat of persecution.

19. It is the scholarly consensus, based on analysis of Mark 4 and 13, that the Gospel addresses a community dealing with the various trials and tribulations that accompany persecution, including struggles within the community over the sorts of conduct that persecution elicits, namely, betrayal, denial of one's faith (apostasy), and the need for forgiveness and reconciliation in the aftermath of such conduct. Mark 13:9, 11–13 affords the clearest evidence for the historical circumstances in and for which Mark was written. There Jesus foresees persecution by both Roman authorities and the synagogue as well as division, even betrayal, within families over allegiance to Jesus and the reign of God. For some scholars the persecution envisioned here points to Rome as the locale of the Markan community and to the cruel assault on Christians initiated by the emperor Nero in the mid-60s. Others argue that such references mirror more closely the savage events of the Roman-Judean war. Wherever the Markan community was located—Rome, Syria, or Galilee—the content of Mark 13 suggests it was living through a time of violence and upheaval that would invite an apocalyptic interpretation such as that on the lips of Jesus in this chapter.

20. John Howard Yoder, *The Politics of Jesus* (Grand Rapids, MI: Eerdmans, 1972), 132. Similarly, noting that "the association of the cross with human suffering has often perverted the Christian life," Stanley Hauerwas maintains that "not only does it encourage some unwisely to accept avoidable suffering, but from a theological point of view it makes us think all our suffering is akin to Christ's. But suffering or even self-sacrifice is not a virtue for Christians when that suffering or sacrifice is not formed by Christ's cross" (Hauerwas, *Suffering Presence*, 31–32).

21. To make the case that renouncing self in 8:34 means, in effect, renouncing one's kinship group, Dewey cites similar sayings in Q (Lk 14:26–27) and the Gospel of Thomas (55 and 101) where the denial of kin is explicit. The link between renunciation of one's kinship group, participation in a new fictive kinship group, and persecution is also evident in Mark 10:29–30. See Dewey, "Let Them Renounce Themselves and Take Up Their Cross," 33–35.

22. Yoder, *The Politics of Jesus*, 132.

23. In the imperial context in which Mark is written, Jesus' reference to current rulers—"among the Gentiles those whom they recognize as

their rulers" (10:42)—includes a subtle but immensely significant assertion that is recognizable in the Greek. The Greek *hoi dokountes archein
tōn ethnōn* should be translated "those of the Gentiles seeming to rule,"
in other words, the supposed rulers, the implication being that it is God
who truly rules.

24. See Hisako Kinukawa, *Women and Jesus in Mark: A Japanese
Feminist Perspective* (Maryknoll, NY: Orbis Books, 1994) 34; and Fran-
ces Taylor Gench, *Back to the Well: Women's Encounters with Jesus in
the Gospels* (Louisville, KY: Westminster/John Knox Press, 2004), 45–46.

25. For enlightening comments regarding the woman's condition in
the context of ancient medicine, see Mary Rose D'Angelo, "Gender and
Power in the Gospel of Mark: The Daughter of Jairus and the Woman
with the Flow of Blood," in *Miracles in Jewish and Christian Antiquity*,
ed. John C. Cavadini, 83–109 (Notre Dame, IN: University of Notre
Dame Press, 1999).

26. See the comments of Karta A. Barta, "'She Spent All She Had . . .
But Only Grew Worse': Paying the Price of Paternalism," in *Where Can
We Find Her? Searching for Women's Identity in the Church*, ed. Marie-
Eloise Rosenblatt, 24–36 (New York: Paulist Press, 1991).

27. Jewish scholars rightly observe that Christian interpreters of this
episode have a tendency to overstate the degree of social ostracism
occasioned by Levitical laws, and in so doing, perpetuate, however
inadvertently, an inaccurate picture of the Jewish world from which
Jesus came. See Shaye J. D. Cohen, "Menstruants and the Sacred in
Judaism and Christianity," in *Women's History and Ancient History*, ed.
Sarah B. Pomeroy, 273–99 (Chapel Hill: University of North Carolina
Press, 1991); Amy-Jill Levine, "Discharging Responsibility: Matthean
Jesus, Biblical Law, and Hemorrhaging Woman," in *Treasures New and
Old: Recent Contributions to Matthean Studies*, ed. David R. Bauer and
Mark Allan Powell, 379–97 (Atlanta: Scholars Press, 1996), reprinted in
Amy-Jill Levine, ed., with Marianne Blickenstaff, *A Feminist Companion
to Matthew* (Sheffield, UK: Sheffield Academic, 2001), 70–87; Paula
Fredriksen, "Did Jesus Oppose the Purity Laws?" *Bible Review* 11 (1995):
20–25, 42–45. See also Charlotte Fonrobert, "The Woman with a Blood-
Flow (Mark 5:25–34) Revisited: Menstrual Laws and Jewish Culture in
Christian Feminist Hermeneutics," in *Early Christian Interpretation of the
Scriptures of Israel: Investigations and Proposals*, ed. Craig A. Evans and
James A. Sanders, *Journal for the Study of the New Testament*, Supple-
ment Series 148 (Sheffield, UK: Sheffield Academic, 1997).

28. For insights into the challenges that those suffering from chronic illness and their families experience, see Kleinman, *The Illness Narratives*, 88–186.

29. Joanna Dewey, "Jesus' Healings of Women: Conformity and Non-Conformity to Dominant Cultural Values as Clues for Historical Reconstruction," in *Society of Biblical Literature 1993 Seminar Papers 38*, ed. Eugene H. Lovering, Jr. (Atlanta: Scholars Press, 1993), 186–88.

30. Jesus' clothes are clearly not possessed of magical properties, for Jesus is fully aware that power has gone forth "from him." The power that the woman's touch accesses is the power of the Holy Spirit that descends from the heavens and enters Jesus at his baptism, empowering him from on high for messianic mission (1:9–11).

31. Mitzi Minor, "Old Stories Through New Eyes: Insights Gained from a Feminist Reading of Mark 5:25–34," *Memphis Theological Seminary Journal* 30 (1992): 9.

32. Arthur Frank (*The Wounded Storyteller*) observes that "seriously ill people are wounded not just in body but in voice. They need to become storytellers in order to recover their voices that illness and its treatment often take away" (xii). He continues, "Stories have to repair the damage that illness has done to the ill person's sense of where she is in life, and where she may be going" (53). "The ill person needs to reaffirm that his story is worth listening to by others" (56). These observations, I suggest, can enrich our appreciation of the significance of the woman's storytelling in her healing encounter with Jesus.

33. The movement that occurs in the woman's story—from isolation to filial relationship—bears reflection in light of Arthur Frank's observation that "the pedagogy of suffering begins its teaching from a ground of loneliness seeking communion" (*The Wounded Storyteller*, 153). Frank's comment also powerfully illumines Jesus' cry from the cross (15:34).

34. D'Angelo, "Gender and Power in the Gospel of Mark," 101.

35. In Mark's narrative logic, this remarkable attitude derives from his conviction, implied by the "must" of the first passion-resurrection prediction, that what he will undergo is willed by God. His statements in the Last Supper episode with their reference to "as it is written" (14:21, 27) and in Gethsemane (14:36) also interpret his destiny as willed by God.

36. In biblical thought the human person is flesh and spirit, but it is the flesh that is vulnerable to pain and death, and so, vulnerable to temptation (*peirasmos),* in this case, the temptation to flee in fear, which for Jesus would mean abandoning the "way of the Lord" (1:2–3) willed by the

Father. Such temptation is simultaneously a test or trial, the other two meanings of *peirasmos*, for the prospect of pain and suffering that tempts one to flee in fear simultaneously serves to test one's fidelity to and trust in God and God's will.

37. The disciples, however, fail to heed the Master's counsel, as three times Jesus finds them not awake and praying but asleep. And so, later in the scene, their willing spirits falter under the weakness of the flesh as they flee, abandoning Jesus in order to save themselves (14:50).

38. In biblical tradition *cup* often symbolizes the fixed amount of whatever God has to offer a person. In the prophets and psalms the image of emptying a cup is used for the suffering that must be endured (see Is 51:17, 22; Jer 25:15; 49:12; 51:7; Hb 2:16; Ps 11:6; 75:9).

39. Christians, however, are not comfortable with lamentation and complaint; such speech strikes us, variously, as whining, impertinence, or a sign of lack of faith. Biblical scholars and pastoral theologians, having noted a neglect of the lament form in Christian liturgical assemblies, are now calling for a recovery of this form of prayer. Their work suggests that praying the laments in the liturgical assembly is a necessary means of facing, with one another and with our God, what is not right in our lives and world. Brueggemann has clarified what is at stake: "A community of faith which negates laments soon concludes that the hard issues of justice are improper questions to pose at the throne, because the throne seems to be only a place of praise. . . . If justice questions are improper at the throne (which is a conclusion drawn through liturgical use), they soon appear to be improper questions in public places, in schools, in hospitals, with the government, and eventually in the courts. Justice questions disappear into civility and docility. The order of the day comes to seem absolute, beyond question, and we are left with only grim obedience and eventually despair" (Walter Brueggemann, "The Costly Loss of Lament," *Journal for the Study of the Old Testament* 36 [1986]: 64). The laments are also a valuable but underused resource for Christian ministries of care, such as work with victims of sexual assault or domestic violence. See Sally Brown and Patrick D. Miller eds., *Lament: Reclaiming Practices in Pulpit, Pew, and Public Square* (Louisville, KY: Westminster/John Knox, 2005).

40. Given Jesus' conviction that his suffering, dying, and rising as Son of Man is the will of God, what he experiences to be the absence of God as he plunges into the "mystery" creates for him a kind of "epistemological crisis," to use Alasdair MacIntyre's term, hence, his "Why . . . ?" On the "epistemological crisis" created by suffering, see Mark J. Hanson,

"Bioethics and the Challenge of Theodicy," in Mohrmann and Hanson, *Pain Seeking Understanding*, 176–77.

41. The Markan interpretation of Jesus' death is found on the lips of Jesus during the journey to Jerusalem—"For the Son of Man must suffer, die, and after three days rise" (8:31; 9:31; 10:33–34) and "The Son of Man came not to be served but to serve, and to give his life as a ransom for many" (10:45)—and at the Last Supper—"This is my blood of the covenant, which is poured out for many" (14:24).

42. In his treatment of the lament psalms Brueggemann contends that "in both complaints concerning failed human hesed [steadfast love] and unresponsive Yahweh, the issue is justice"; moreover, that by their regular use, Israel kept the justice questions alive and legitimate. See Brueggemann, "The Costly Loss of Lament," 57–71, esp. 63.

43. Brueggemann contends that this form of prayer-speech attests to the courage and ego-strength with which Israel came before Yahweh in prayer; furthermore, that these prayers testify that God wills to relate to "a responsible, mature covenant partner who can enter into serious communion and conversation. In such a serious conversation and communion, there comes genuine obedience, which is not a contrived need to please, but a genuine, yielding commitment" ("Costly Loss," 61).

44. In narrative context this silence and lack of reply does not mean that Abba has abandoned and is not present to Jesus' anguish. Immediately upon Jesus' death the Temple veil is torn (15:38). In narrative and cultural context, this may be read a number of ways. I suggest that it is, among other things, a sign that Abba has been moved by the Son's desperate cry and is on the move. That divine movement is confirmed by the subsequent resurrection (16:1–8), where "he has been raised" *(ēgerthē)* is another theological passive, indicating an act of God.

45. Wendy Farley, "The Practice of Theodicy," in Mohrmann and Hanson, *Pain Seeking Understanding*, 112.

46. Walter Kasper, *The God of Jesus Christ* (New York: Crossroad, 1984), 84. On suffering in a mystical-political spirituality, see Kristine M. Rankka, *Women and the Value of Suffering: An Aw(e)ful Rowing Toward God* (Collegeville, MN: Liturgical Press, 1998).

PART II

CONTEMPORARY THEOLOGICAL REFLECTION ON SUFFERING

FOUR

The Divine Purpose
and Human Suffering

Richard W. Miller

In the face of the suffering of the world, Epicurus's old and unanswered questions spontaneously well up within us,

> Is he [God] unwilling to prevent evil, but not
> able? Then he is impotent.
> Is he able, but not willing? Then is he malevo-
> lent.
> Is he both able and willing? Whence then is
> evil?[1]

In our times David Hume's Epicurean questions have been condensed into a couplet in Archibald MacLeish's play *J.B.*:

> If God is God, he is not good
> If God is good, he is not God.[2]

Evil and *suffering* are ambiguous terms and thus are often used interchangeably. In this essay evil will be understood as that which is destructive to the human being, while suffering adds the aspect of the experience of that evil. If a doctor assists a person in committing suicide, what is done is destructive and evil, but the person does not continue to suffer. In fact, the destructive

83

or evil act is carried out in order to avoid suffering. In addition, it is important to note that not all suffering is destructive. For instance, a person might suffer from a medical operation, but the operation itself is not destructive; it is intended to heal the person. Moreover, the person who goes through the spiritual night of the senses and the spiritual night of the soul certainly suffers, but this suffering is not destructive but purgative. Suffering in this essay refers to the experience of that which is destructive to the human being.

In responding to Epicurus's old and unanswered questions, we will be leaving the close analysis of Old Testament and New Testament texts on suffering that my colleagues in biblical theology have provided in order to approach the problem of suffering in Christian life through systematic theology. Systematic theology is a discipline in theology that relates doctrines and Christian mysteries to each other so that they can be mutually illuminating and enrich our thinking. For instance, if we relate the doctrine of the incarnation, that God so loved the world that the second Person of the Triune God became fully human, to theological anthropology then we can better glimpse the dignity and eternal significance of the human being. A similar enrichment of our thinking happens when we relate the doctrine of the incarnation to the doctrine of creation. If the Infinite became finite and entered into human history, which is coterminous with the history of the natural world, then we can better glimpse the dignity and the significance of the whole created order.

The task of relating doctrines can draw upon many different disciplines, but preeminently it draws upon philosophy. Philosophical theology, as a subset of systematic theology, not only helps to disclose the richness and plumb the depths of various doctrines through relating them to one another, but also aids in establishing, clarifying, and demonstrating the coherence of theological statements.

The method of systematic theology, including philosophical theology as a subset of systematic theology, was the method recommended by the First Vatican Council,

If reason illumined by faith inquires in an earnest, pious and sober manner, it attains by God's grace a certain understanding of the mysteries, which is most fruitful, both from the analogy with the objects of its natural knowledge and from the connection of these mysteries with one another and with our ultimate end.[3]

In this essay I approach the problem of God and human suffering by bringing aspects of the doctrine of God, guided by the content of faith and aided by philosophical principles (natural knowledge), into dialogue with theological anthropology and the last end of the human being. This essay has four parts: (1) An elucidation of the proper understanding of the concept of mystery as applied to God. This includes a clarification of why the theodicy problem is not a problem that human beings can master but is an aspect of the enduring mystery of God in which "we live and move and have our being" (Acts 17:28). (2) In light of the mystery of God and the concomitant limits to human knowledge I formulate the most foundational or most basic question for all further reflection regarding the problem of human suffering and belief in a God of infinite wisdom, goodness, and power. (3) I respond to this foundational question through an examination of created freedom in relationship to the created person's end. (4) I show how the conclusions from the analysis of created persons relate to the problem of human suffering from nature (tsunamis, plagues, and so on) and the question of God intervening (special divine action) to prevent human suffering.

God as Mystery

The concept mystery as applied to God indicates the limits of human knowledge and as such counters any facile and overconfident rationalism when approaching the theodicy question. Indeed, the concept of mystery as applied to God indicates that God cannot be fully comprehended. The concept of mystery, however, cannot simply be employed to indicate the limits of human knowledge.

While Christianity is not rationalistic in its knowledge of God, it is also not agnostic in its knowledge of God. John's Gospel, for instance, describes eternal life as the knowledge of the one true God and Jesus Christ whom the Father has sent (Jn 17: 3–4).

The concept mystery indicates that human beings can know God but cannot comprehend God. God is not incomprehensible because God is unknowable like a contradiction (for example, male sisters). For something is knowable to the degree that it "is." You and I are more knowable than less complex beings in the hierarchy of being, like primary particles that pulse in and out of existence. And God, as the fullness of existence and life, is that reality that is most knowable. God is not incomprehensible to us because God is unknowable like a hypothetical reality that cannot be known by us because of its distance from us. For example, the existence of intelligent life in other galaxies cannot be known by us because of the immense distances between us and those other galaxies. The central message of Christianity, I suggest, is that God has communicated God's self to human beings so that human beings can share in God's eternal life. God in God's self is present to us. We do know God. Thus when we say that God is mystery we cannot, in a Christian account, maintain that God is incomprehensible because God is a contradiction or that God is incomprehensible because God is removed and distant from us. Rather, God is knowable and more present to us than we are to ourselves. God, however, is infinite, and we are finite. While not distant from creatures, God is "Other" than us. God is incomprehensible not because God is unknowable, but because God as Infinite cannot be grasped fully by us. And thus God cannot be known by us to the full extent that God is knowable. God is inexhaustibly knowable. The term *mystery* when it is applied to God, means that God, who has shared Godself with human beings, is incomprehensible because God is inexhaustibly intelligible.

Our experience of God as mystery is an enduring aspect of our relationship to God. While the promise of Christianity is that we will share in God's life in union with God in the beatific vision, we will always be finite creatures and God is eternally infinite.[4] The distinction between the Infinite God and the finite creature is not overcome in the vision of God. God remains incomprehensible in the beatific vision because the human being continues to be finite. The creature does not become the infinite God.[5] As such the creature in union with God will know God, but will not know as God knows. The creature will not know infinitely.[6] Thus the theodicy problem along with all theological problems are not problems that human beings can master; rather, they are aspects of the enduring mystery of God in which "we live and move and have our being" (Acts 17:28). One of the central tasks of the theologian is to preserve the understanding of God as mystery (as inexhaustibly intelligible). This task involves a twofold process. First, the theologian must ensure that his or her theologizing is consistently cognizant of the incomprehensibility of God by articulating the limited range of human knowledge of God. Second, the theologian must ensure that his or her theologizing is consistently cognizant of the intelligibility of God by resolving any contradictions that fall within this limited range of human knowledge of God.

God as Mystery and the Limits of Human Knowledge: In Search of the Foundational Question

The theodicy question as formulated by David Hume involves a host of secondary questions concerning God's omniscience, omnipotence, and omnibenevolence. In this section of the essay I continue to probe the limits of human knowledge by examining our knowledge of God in relation to God's freedom. This analysis leads to a formulation of the most foundational or most basic question for all further reflection regarding the problem of human suffering and belief in a God of infinite wisdom, goodness, and power.

When we say speak of God's essential attributes—existence, goodness, truth, oneness, beauty—we are making true statements without comprehending their full meaning. We must recognize and constantly remind ourselves that all of our theological statements are incomprehensible, and thus mystery conditions everything we say about God. These attributes—existence, goodness, truth, oneness, beauty—are the absolutely transcendental properties of being,[7] which are attributes that are common to every being in so far as it is (the transcendentals). These attributes pertain to the divine substance. A second type of attributes pertains to the divine operation.[8] The second type of attributes (the transcendental relative properties of being) is not derived from the very fact that something is. As such these attributes are not coextensive with all being; rather, they are perfections analogously derived from the human being. Thus, God as the infinite and perfect source of all being must possess these perfections (knowledge, love, and so forth). The limits of human knowledge become even more profound when we reflect upon those attributes of God that pertain to God's activity, especially in relation to human beings and the created universe (God's ominiscience, omnipotence, and omnibenevolence).

Here I focus on the limits of human knowledge by reflecting on God's freedom. In speaking of God's freedom we are trying to preserve the divine perfection in two senses: God's freedom of exercise and God's freedom of specification. God's freedom of exercise indicates that God did not create the universe or give God's self (grace) out of need or a necessity of nature. God did not create the universe and communicate God's self in order to be God. If God needed to create the universe to achieve God's perfection, then God would not be essentially perfect. God would not be creating out of love but out of need, and thus God would need the universe to be God. As such, God would not be perfect. Rather, God creates, sustains the universe in being, and gives God's self out of sheer gratuity; God wants to share God's life with us.

God's freedom of specification indicates that this universe does not exhaust God's perfection. It is a finite universe. God could have created a different universe. The universe does not exhaust God's infinite perfection. Let me provide an example to clarify this point. We exalt Michelangelo Buonarroti (1475–1564) as one of the great geniuses in Western civilization. An indication of Michelangelo's perfection is that his talent seemed inexhaustible. He mastered multiple disciplines—sculpture, painting, architecture, poetry, and engineering—and continued to be productive throughout his life. More specifically, his perfection and greatness were revealed by the fact that no single artwork exhausted his creative capacity. For instance, sculpting the magnificent David (1501–4) did not exhaust his creativity. He went on to paint the Sistine Chapel ceiling (1508–12), the Last Judgment fresco (1534–41) in the Sistine Chapel, and a host of other artistic achievements, including contributing to the design of St. Peter's Basilica (1546–64). The David sculpture, as wonderful as it is, did not exhaust Michelangelo's perfection. Analogously, the universe, as grand as it is (scientists speculate that there are one thousand billion billion stars) does not exhaust the perfection of God. The universe in all its magnificence is still finite. God is infinite.

God in knowing God's self and in rejoicing in God's self knows that God's being can be shared with others. God wills to bring creatures into being so that they can share or participate in God's being and life. Thus the purpose of God's activity (at a minimum) outside the inner life of the Trinity is to share God's self with a community of the blessed in the beatific vision.[9] In light of this purpose, there is a corollary to what I have argued regarding God's freedom of specification; namely, God could have achieved God's purpose by creating and giving God's self in grace to a different universe than this one. Because of this we cannot know why God created this universe, and even more specifically we cannot know why God created this planet with its earthquakes, tsunamis, disease, and so on.

The limits of human knowledge of God's free choice are not only applicable to our knowledge of the kind of universe God created but also to the particular ways God acts within the universe. Although Christian belief holds that God guides nature and history out of God's infinite wisdom, goodness, and power, one cannot have access to the particular free acts of God unless God chooses to disclose the reason for those acts. Examples of God disclosing the reason for God's acts can be seen in the Gospels' different accounts of the purpose of the coming of Jesus Christ. In Mark 10:45 and Matthew 20:28 the purpose of the coming of the Son of Man is "to serve, and to give his life as a ransom for many."[10] In Luke 19:10 the Son of Man comes to seek out and save the outcasts and the lost. And in John 10:10 the Son comes into the world so human beings "may have life, and have it abundantly," for, "God so loved the world that he gave his only Son, so that everyone who believes in him may not perish but may have eternal life" (Jn 3:16). The reason for the particular free acts of God must be revealed to us because the free acts of God are contingent and thus could be otherwise. God could act in a number of different ways, and thus we cannot know why God permits suffering in a particular instance.

When we say that God permits suffering, we are assuming that God can intervene to prevent suffering. Although the phrase *divine intervention* is commonly used, it is problematic because it suggests that God is "out there somewhere" and reaches into the natural world and history to right the direction of events. God, however, is not "out there somewhere." There is no place that God is not; God is omnipresent. All metaphors of outside and inside fall radically short because God is everywhere. God is the ground and source of all being. These metaphors, however, can be useful to distinguish God and the world as long as we simultaneously recognize their limitations. A more adequate way of speaking is to talk about God acting in a special particular way (special divine action) to guide nature and history to its end. *Special divine action* is a more precise phrase that indicates that God can act in a mode above and beyond God's sustaining a creature in being (conservation) and applying a creature to act according to its nature (governance). It would take us too far afield to examine the difficult question of miracles and how to interpret the miracles in the New Testament. We, however, are on safer theological ground not to rule out the possibility that God can act in a special way. If we assume that God can act in a special particular way it raises the question: why does God permit suffering? Yet we cannot know why God permits suffering in a particular instance. We also cannot know if God has intervened (special divine action) unbeknown to the person, in other instances to prevent suffering.

The theologian also cannot know the particular character of God's loving response to other people in the throes of suffering. We can know that it is a loving response through the effect of God's action in ourselves, in witnessing the effect in others, through others communicating to us their experience of being given strength, courage and peace in the midst of suffering, or the unexpected good that emerged in the wake of the destructive event. We cannot, however, know why God freely chose to respond, among all the possible ways God could have responded to us, in exactly this way to our suffering and thus produced these particular effects in us.

This outline of the limits of human knowledge raises a question: what kind of knowledge can a theologian have? The knowledge a theologian can have is a general knowledge grounded in God's twofold self-disclosure in creation and revelation. Through revelation we know (although not comprehensively) the purpose or end of God's creating and offering God's self to human beings. Because we know the end, we can make theological judgments about the conditions that must be necessary if God has made this end possible for human beings. This is knowledge arrived at through hypothetical necessity. If a particular end is to be reached, then by necessity certain conditions must obtain (if C is to exist, then A and B must exist). God has freedom of exercise and does not have to create and grace this universe. If God does create and grace this universe and the end or purpose of this universe is known through revelation, then certain conditions are necessary. More precisely, if the purpose of God's creating the universe is to give God's self to creatures (created persons) so that they can be united with God and share in the fullness of God's life, then certain conditions must obtain for this end to be truly possible.

These necessary conditions are the intelligible context within which God creates, sustains, and governs this universe. In other words, God's will operates in the context of the possible (intelligible) ways in which God's being and life can be communicated to creatures.[11] To say that God's freedom is conditioned by what is possible does not mean we have limited God's freedom and power and thus undermined God's omnipotence, for what is possible is dictated by God's being. That God's freedom is necessarily orientated to the intelligibility of God's being as communicable is integral to God's perfection. If God's freedom is not necessarily *related* to the intelligibility of God's being, then God's will would be absolute. If the divine will is understood as absolute, then God's activity would not be guided by the intelligibility of God's being as communicable (the divine goodness) and God could act arbitrarily and God could in God's good pleasure do terrible things. God is not more perfect for having the capacity to do what cannot be done, to act unintelligibly, or to act capriciously. God's will is not absolute; it is relative to the intelligibility of God's being as communicable. This does not contradict the perfection of God's will; rather, it is intrinsic to the perfection of God's will.

To this point I have situated the question of this chapter within the overall problematic of the apparent contradiction between the reality of human suffering and belief in a God of infinite wisdom, goodness, and power. Let me summarize the moments of this argument. First, an essential part of the task of treating the problem of God and human suffering is to preserve the mystery of God. Second, mystery as attributed to God must be understood in terms of inexhaustible intelligibility. Third, we cannot know why God permits suffering in this particular instance or the character of God's response to someone in the throes of suffering. We can know in a general way, however, the necessary conditions of the possibility for the realization of God's purpose (hypothetical necessity) because we know the purpose of God's activity through revelation.

It follows from this threefold argument that when we address the problematic of human suffering and belief in a God of infinite wisdom, goodness, and power from the perspective of preserving the mystery of God, we must begin with the purpose of God's creative and salvific activity and frame the question in terms of hypothetical necessity. The recognition of the limits of our knowledge reveals the foundational or most basic question for all further reflection regarding the problem of human suffering and belief in a God of infinite wisdom, goodness, and power; namely, if God created the universe in order to give God's self to creatures so that they could be united with God and share in the fullness of God's life, could God have achieved this purpose without *any* suffering of created persons?

Two additional assumptions that are operative here further focus our reflections. First, following Thomas Aquinas and Karl Rahner, I assume that God can only give God's self to created spirits (more properly, as we will see, created persons). What does it mean to be a created spirit? Let us compare the human being to another animal, the polar bear. The range of the experience of polar bears is circumscribed by their senses. While polar bears' eyesight is probably equal in range to human beings, polar bears can detect prey through their sense of smell from up to twenty miles away. While this is quite impressive, the range of polar bears' experience is determined by sensation. The range of human beings' experience as spirits, more precisely as spirits in matter, is not utterly constrained by their senses. Human beings can ask questions. While I exist at this particular place and time, I can ask questions about the whole universe going back 13.7 billion years to its origins. I can ask questions about all that exists. As such, I am open to the totality of being as true and good, including God. Because I am open by nature to all that exists, including God, I have the potential to share in God's life, should God choose to actualize this potential.[12] In other words, the condition of the possibility of my sharing in God's eternal life in the beatific vision is that I am a created spirit open to all that is, including God.

The second assumption that is operative here is that it was possible for God to bring into being two types of created spirits—human beings and immaterial spirits or angels.[13] Reflecting on whether angels exist or not and their theological significance would take us too far afield. What is relevant here is that in light of our limited knowledge we do not want to restrict the possibilities open to God, and so we allow for the possibility of angels. If we accept the possibility of two kinds of created spirits, then if God created in order to give God's self to creatures so that they could be united with God and share in the fullness of God's life, it is possible, in light of God's freedom of specification, that God did not have to create a universe of embodied spirits or human beings. It is possible that God could have created a universe of immaterial spirits or angels and achieved God's purpose. We cannot know why God created this universe and thus why God created embodied spirits (human beings) who are subject to all the suffering involved in being embodied—diseases, earthquakes, and so on. All that can be said is that if God wanted to achieve God's end of sharing God's self in union with creatures, then God had to create spiritual beings.

Thus, while this essay is concerned with the suffering of human beings and comes out of the experience of human beings, the only way to address this question, respecting the limits of human knowledge, is to address the question of human suffering insofar as human beings are created spirits or more properly (as will be shown in this essay) created persons. While this examination of the necessary conditions of the possibility (the hypothetical necessity) of God sharing God's self with created persons will be unavoidably abstract, it should be kept in mind that its real concern is with the concrete existential situation of human life.

A great deal is at stake in this question: if God created the universe in order to give God's self to creatures so that they could be united with God and share in the fullness of God's life, could God have achieved this purpose without *any* suffering of created persons? If God could have achieved God's creative and salvific purpose without *any* of the pain and suffering of human history, including the suffering of Christ, then the eternal plan of providence and the actual unfolding of salvation history would be arbitrary and irrational. God would not be inexhaustibly intelligible, but God and God's activity would be absurd.

The Divine Purpose and Created Freedom

Since our question deals with the conditions of the possibility of God realizing God's creative and salvific purpose of giving God's self to created persons, we must begin by asking about the conditions necessary for God giving God's self in union to created persons. This entails an examination of the freedom of created persons by examining created freedom in terms of its end or final cause. In beginning with created freedom, I initially approach the issue of suffering in terms of the destructive suffering of created persons that results from their free choice. I first examine human freedom and then relate analogically this understanding of human freedom to the freedom of the other type of created persons (angels). I will thus outline the basic characteristics of all created freedom such that if God is going to create spirits, they will necessarily have these basic characteristics.

If the will were not necessarily ordered to an end, the will would not be capable of acting. Action requires a determinate end. If an agent were not necessarily oriented to some definite end, then it would be, at its root, indifferent. From an agent utterly indifferent to various ends, no action can result, for there would be no reason for the agent to act.[14] For instance, if I were not oriented by nature toward self-preservation, then I would be indifferent to eating and drinking and there would be no reason for me to act in ways to ensure my survival. If I am not oriented by nature toward any reality, then I would be indifferent to everything and as such there would be no reason for me to act at all. If there is no reason for me to act, then I would not act.

If the will were not oriented by nature toward God as the Infinite Good, then human beings would not be capable of acts of free choice. For instance, if I were oriented by nature to a particular action like playing tennis, I would always play tennis. I would not be able to choose to play soccer, basketball, or to read. I would engage only in this finite and limited good activity of playing tennis. Conversely, if human beings are orientated toward the Infinite Good, that reality that contains within itself all possible goods that one could ever desire, then no finite and limited good will fully satisfy us. No finite good—playing tennis, playing soccer, reading—will fully satisfy me. Since these finite goods will never satisfy me, I have a choice among them. If any one of them would fully satisfy me, I would immediately move toward it by nature. It doesn't fully satisfy me, though, so now I have choices among them, and I have to weigh what I would like to do: Do I prefer to play tennis? Do I prefer to play soccer? Do I prefer to read? It is our necessary orientation to the Infinite Good that allows us to have the power to choose among finite goods. Since the will is ordered toward the Infinite Good and finite goods are not good without limit, then the will is not compelled to choose a particular finite good. As such, the will has free choice among finite goods. It is, according to W. Norris Clarke, "the deeper necessity within us toward the Infinite which sets us free toward the finite."[15]

This orientation to the Infinite Good is expressed in the human being's restless desire for God. The most famous statement of this central component of human experience comes from Saint Augustine in his *Confessions*—"You have made us for Yourself and our hearts are restless 'til they rest in You."[16] This desire for God as the Infinite Good is constitutive of who we are and permeates all of our experience. In everything we desire we implicitly desire God. All things are created and sustained in being by God, and they reflect, in a limited way, the goodness of their Infinite Source. Because these finite goods reflect the goodness of their Infinite Cause, we are attracted to them. Because these goods are finite and not the Infinite Good, none of them will quiet our restlessness. Even the greatest of goods will not fully quell our desires. For example, while marriage is one of the great goods of human life as the highest form of friendship, marriage will not fully quench our yearnings. Married life might be wonderful and exceed our expectations; nevertheless, marriage will not fully satisfy us. It will not quell the human heart. One indication of this is that we continue to desire other goods—knowledge, health, and so on. If we think that marriage will fully satisfy us, and we enter into marriage with this disposition and rigidly cling to this disposition, we will destroy the marriage. Nothing finite, even a wonderful and holy human being, can fully satisfy another human being. That doesn't mean that they are awful and terrible because they cannot fulfill our desires; no, they really are good. But they are not God, and "our hearts are restless until they rest in God."

In seeking the Infinite Good, human beings choose finite goods as partial means toward the achievement of their final end, the Good in itself. Because we are not in full union with God in this life, in our desire for happiness and fulfillment we pursue particular finite goods because they reflect, in a limited way, the goodness of their Infinite Source that we long for. God is the only thing that can satisfy us, but we cannot grasp God directly in this life so we become ourselves and determine who we are by the way we relate to other finite beings in space and time.

If we hold that the intelligibility of free choice requires that the human being is necessarily orientated toward the Infinite God, then we must say that in the beatific vision the intellectual creature no longer has free choice vis-à-vis God. If we by nature long for union with God and implicitly desire God in all of our choices, then it would not make sense that we would have the capacity to choose something other than God if God elevates us into God's presence at the moment of our death. If we are implicitly and necessarily seeking the Infinite Good as our end and perfection, as the total Good that contains within itself all possible goods that we could ever desire, then if we should be presented (through the light of glory) with the Infinite Good we would necessarily embrace it.[17] We would not be free to choose or not to choose the Infinite Good. We would necessarily "embrace it with the total spontaneous power of our wills, as that which we have always implicitly wanted and longed for with the deepest longing of our very nature."[18] For, as W. Norris Clarke rightly maintains:

> What sense could it possibly make for my will actually to be presented with the Absolute Good in itself, seen clearly as my good, what I really have wanted all the time and yet not to choose it but to choose some lesser finite good instead, whose goodness is already contained in super-eminent fashion in the original Source?[19]

The spontaneous and necessary embrace of the Infinite Good in the immediate presence of God is the perfection of freedom *(libertas)*. Here there is no place for freedom of choice *(liberum arbitrium)* in relationship to our ultimate end, for free choice "would be replaced by a total, voluntary, spontaneous 'yes' welling up from and giving definitive expression to the most radical dynamism of our will as nature."[20] This spontaneous action is an unrestrained expression of the human being's graced nature in its dynamic orientation toward the Infinite Good. If this voluntary spontaneous acceptance of the Infinite Good is the perfection of freedom *(libertas)*, then free choice *(liberum arbitrium)* is the power to determine for oneself the means to one's ultimate end. Free choice is "a means only to the attainment of the fuller and more perfect freedom which the will must attain if it is to achieve its perfection."[21] As such, free choice *(liberum arbitrium)* vis-à-vis God, as a means to the perfection of freedom *(libertas),* "would be transcended and left behind"[22] when the human being reached its end, the perfected state of freedom *(libertas)*.

In the presence of the Infinite Good, the will would not only spontaneously embrace the Infinite Good as its end but would also unwaveringly adhere to the Infinite Good as its end. This is because the free creature could not desire a finite good as opposed to the Infinite Good, for the goodness of the particular finite good is contained super-eminently in the Infinite Good. If the free creature unwaveringly adheres to the Infinite Good, then the person would be incapable of acting wrongly.[23] Thus, in the perfection of freedom, sin, moral evil, moral imperfection, and error are impossible.[24]

Does a Proper Understanding of Created Freedom Exacerbate the Problem of God and Human Suffering?

If the perfection of freedom is a state in which the will necessarily embraces and unwaveringly adheres to the Infinite Good, then could not God have created free creatures by nature such that they would necessarily adhere to the Infinite Good? In addition, could not God have created intellectual creatures with free choice *(liberum arbitrium)* and then immediately elevated them through the light of glory such that they would embrace God and be in the possession of their end (the beatific vision) through the first acts of their intellect and will? In either one of these scenarios of unwavering adherence to the Infinite Good, creatures would be incapable of sin, moral imperfection, moral evil, or error. Thus it appears that God could have achieved God's purpose without any suffering. If God could have achieved God's purpose without any suffering, then it is hard to see how God could be the loving God of Jesus Christ.

Let us examine the first scenario—if the perfection of freedom is a state in which the will necessarily embraces and unwaveringly adheres to the Infinite Good, could God have created free creatures by nature such that they would necessarily adhere to the Infinite Good? God, in knowing and loving, knows and loves God's self as the end and all created things as ordered to God's self as their end. God is supremely active, and the end of God's activity is God. Thus the rule and measure of God's actions is God. Fault in the will is not possible where the agent is identical with the rule, as in God. Thomas Aquinas uses the image of a craftsman to illustrate this point: "If the craftsman's hand were itself the rule of cutting, then the craftsman could not cut the wood otherwise than rightly; but if the rightness of engraving be judged by another rule, then the engraving may be right or faulty. Now the divine will is the only rule of God's act because it is not ordered to any higher end."[25] Free creatures, on the other hand, by the very fact that they are created, are subject to another as to rule and measure.[26] The free creature is referred to God as its end, and God is an end that is both other than it and higher than it. A free creature has "rectitude in its act only to the extent that it is regulated according to the Divine will, to which its ultimate end pertains *(pertinet)*."[27] The free creature necessarily desires the Infinite Good, but has to determine itself within by choosing means to that end. In proportioning means to an end, which is both other than it and higher than it, the free creature is capable of fault. God, then, could not create free creatures who by nature always act rightly.

Let us review the second scenario. It is true that when the creature is perfectly united to God in the beatific vision it will always act rightly. But a creature cannot be united to God by its own act. God must act upon it to elevate it (through the light of glory). The question then becomes: could God have created intellectual creatures with free choice *(liberum arbitrium)* and then immediately elevated creatures through the light of glory such that they would embrace God and be in the possession of their end (the beatific vision) through the first acts of their intellect and will? In this scenario God could achieve the purpose of the universe (to share

God's self in union with free creatures) without any possibility of moral imperfection, moral evil, sin, and suffering.

At first glance this scenario in no way seems to violate human freedom. Free creatures would not be able to reject God, for they would be presented with God, through God elevating them into the beatific vision in the first instance of their creation, and they would spontaneously embrace God as the One toward whom their nature is dynamically oriented. This state of unwavering adherence to God not only in no way violates human freedom, but, as we have seen, is precisely the perfection of freedom *(libertas)*.

We have seen that in the beatific vision the creature would not have free choice vis-à-vis God. That is to say, if the free creature is elevated into the presence of God, it would spontaneously accept the Infinite Good and would not have free choice to reject the Infinite Good. This does not, however, mean that the created spirit would not have free choice in the vision of God. The free creature would no longer have free choice, understood as the means to achieving its final end or perfection, because it will have already attained its ultimate end. The free creature will, however, have free choice as overflowing from its perfection as united with God in the beatific vision. In the beatific vision the created spirit will not choose in order to possess God, but will choose out of the desire to communicate its perfection, which it has acquired from union with God, to others in the community of the blessed. The free creature in union with God wills nothing outside of itself except as a free communication of its goodness. This is analogous to God's willing, in which God wills nothing outside of God's self except as a free communication of God's goodness. God in knowing God's self knows all the ways in which God's goodness can be communicated. Out of the infinite plenitude of God's goodness, which God knows that God can share, God has free choice. Analogous to the free choice of God, the free creature united with God exists in the perfect state of its distinct and individual created perfection; out of its perfection it is free to choose to communicate its goodness to others in the community of the blessed. As God infinitely wills God's self and all things as ordered to God's self, the free creature in the beatific vision wills, as a creature, itself and all goods it wishes to communicate to others as ordered to God's own goodness, which is the end to which it is united. The free creature will know God and others by participating in the way God knows God's self. This means that the extent and depth of the free creature's relatedness to all things will be far greater in the vision than in its earthly life. In addition, the possibilities open to it for freely communicating its goodness to others will also be far greater in the vision than in its earthly life. The possibility of free choice in the vision of God then will be neither nonexistent nor more constricted than in this present life; rather, it will be far greater in the vision of God.

It appears, then, that God, upon creating the creature, could immediately elevate the creature such that the creature would be united with God through the first acts of its intellect and will without the creature losing the perfection of free choice. Indeed, the creature would possess the perfection of free choice much more fully. If this is true, then God could have given God's self to free creatures so that they could be united with God and share in the fullness of God's life without any possibility of evil and suffering; for free creatures in the vision would have free choice, and they would exercise their choice without any imperfection or fault. It appears, then, that God could have achieved God's creative and salvific purpose without the pain and suffering of human history. Since God obviously did not realize this possibility, it seems that the eternal plan of providence is arbitrary and irrational.

An influential response in the history of theology and philosophy to the theodicy problem is the free-will defense. There are different variations of the free-will defense, but they all tend to assume that created free choice necessarily involves the possibility of immoral and wrongful choices. The basic components of the argument are as follows. First, if human beings are going to have the power of free choice, this entails that they have the possibility to make immoral or wrong choices that inflict suffering. Second, the source of much evil and suffering in the world is human beings making immoral or faulty choices. Third, God is justified in creating creatures with free choice because the possible goods (virtues, the capacity to respond to God's invitation to share in God's eternal life, and so on) outweigh the possible negative consequences resulting from creatures' faulty free choice.

The argument I have presented, however, rules out the free-will defense. It rejects the idea that free choice necessarily entails the possibility of faulty choice. It is, as I have argued, possible to be united to God in the beatific vision and to have free choice; indeed, one would have even greater free choice than one had prior to being united with God. Additional arguments show the inadequacy of understanding free choice as entailing the possibility of faulty choices. If always choosing the good is at odds with what it means to be free, then the moral action of a saint could be considered free only if on occasion the saint acted immorally. Thus the saint habitually choosing the good would make that person less free. As one advanced in perfection, one's capacity for free choice would be diminished. Human perfection and free choice would then be inversely related. A Christian understanding of freedom, however, does not imply the possibility of acting immorally. In fact, true freedom is not compatible with evil choice. In Christian teaching, immoral actions enslave us.

My analysis of the conditions of the possibility of free choice seems to take away one of the best responses Christians had for defending their belief in an all-loving, all-knowing, and all-powerful God in the face of human suffering. While my analysis of free choice makes the theodicy problem considerably worse, it only treats one aspect of the human person and, as such, is incomplete. While I lay out the intelligibility of free choice in terms of the free creature's natural dynamism toward the Infinite, I have not dealt with created personhood. An examination of created personhood will be the key to showing why God could not achieve God's purpose without any human suffering.

Created Personhood

The dynamism of the human being toward Infinite Truth and Goodness indicates the essence of the human being in terms of its potentiality for specific actions (knowing, loving, and so on), which is what is meant by a "nature." We saw that action requires an end. If action requires an end, then an agent's nature indicates the end toward which its being is oriented. A human person, however, is not simply a human nature because when one speaks of human nature one has not yet spoken of the subject itself, for a spiritual nature subsists in a subject. The subsistence of a spiritual nature in a subject is what I mean by *person.* More precisely, a person is "an actual existent [i.e. with its own act of existence], distinct from all others, possessing an intellectual nature."[28] To speak of human nature is to indicate "what I am" (or more precisely, what kind of actor I am). To speak of the human person is to speak of "who I am."[29] If I were to ask you, "What are you?" you would unhesitatingly reply, "I am a human being." If, however, I were to ask you, "Who are you?" you might hesitate, stammer a bit, or even become offended, for the question by a stranger is inappropriate because it is "too personal." It is probing for what is most intimate and unique about you. It is asking for the unique "I" or person that you are.

You would reply to the question—who are you?—by telling your story. That story would inevitably include conditions over which you had no control: the time and location of your birth, the family into which you were born, your particular mental and physical characteristics (talents or deficits), and more. Central to your story would be how you responded through your free choices to the givens of your nature, biological endowment, and historical circumstances. What would be most revelatory of who you are would be the choices you made. It is in one's choices that one simultaneously makes oneself to be this particular person and discloses oneself to oneself and others. For instance, if I choose to steal, I become a thief. By nature we have potential to know and choose. In our actualizing this potential to choose, which follows upon our act of knowing that includes weighing different possibilities for our actions, the person emerges. This particular "I" or person emerges out of the necessities of nature, biology, and history. The person emerges through free choices *in response* to the necessities of nature, biology, and history. It is as a person that

"I" am recognized as having responsibility for my actions; indeed, this responsibility is codified institutionally in our legal system, so that "I" could be held accountable for being a thief.

The analysis of the natural dynamic orientation of the created spirit to the Infinite Good and the analysis of the human person not only holds true for human beings but also for angels. I indicated in my treatment of God's freedom of specification that in order not to restrict the possibilities open to God, I assume that it was possible for God to create a universe of immaterial spirits or angels. If we follow Thomas Aquinas's metaphysics of angels, which he develops analogically through his understanding of being, human beings, and God, then biological necessity and historical circumstances would not be constitutive of an angel. The angel, however, would in the first instance of its creation have to make a single decision about itself as related to the Infinite Good. It would have to choose either to affirm itself as oriented toward the Infinite through surrendering itself to the Infinite or choose to deny its natural orientation toward Infinite Truth and Goodness. Because of the structure of angelic knowledge (which I will not develop because of space constraints), which follows from their immateriality, angels must make a single and irrevocable free choice as to whether or not they unconditionally accept God as their final end. If there are angels, being an angel is a high-stakes game! The human being, on the other hand, gets many chances. We may reverse a decision by adopting a new moral orientation that either reforms our life or conversely debases our life.

The point here in reintroducing immaterial beings or angels is to insist that created spirits—either human beings or possibly angels—must take possession of their natures. Angelic personhood, unlike human personhood, does not emerge in response to biological and historical necessities; angelic personhood, like human personhood, emerges through a response to the necessity of its nature, that is, the angel's necessary orientation to the Infinite Good. Since the created spirit (both human and angel) exists as related toward the Infinite Other, its activity is necessarily a giving or disposing of itself. It is only through its free choice that the creature takes possession of itself and affirms or denies what it is by nature. In denying its natural orientation toward the Infinite, the created spirit constricts itself and measures reality not in relation to Infinite Being and Goodness, but according to itself or some other finite thing. The act of free choice is simultaneously the act by which one possesses oneself in a particular way and the act by which one gives oneself over to the Infinite or to the finite. To give oneself over to the dynamism of one's nature is to find oneself in the presence of God and the fullness of life. Here is the philosophical underpinning of the revealed truth that "only the one who loses himself can find himself" (Mt 10:39). On the other hand, to reject one's natural dynamism to the Infinite Good by absolutizing finite things is to enact a contradiction, one is implicitly affirming one's dynamic orientation to the Infinite Good through one's choice while simultaneously denying one's dynamic orientation to the Infinite Good. The key point is that it is in free choice that a created spirit possesses itself and thus becomes a person.

The intelligibility of free choice entails the fact that when God elevates the free creature into the beatific vision, it will not have free choice in relation to its end. Yet it is through acts of free choice that a human being responds to the necessities of nature, biology, and history to become an "I" or person—a someone who is not reducible to the various necessities. And it is through an act of free choice that an angel responds to the necessities of its nature to become an "I" or person—a someone. It is through their free choice(s) that created spirits actualize the potential of their nature and in so doing constitute themselves as unique persons. This becoming of created persons must occur outside the beatific vision. It is only in the order of grace, where the created spirit must not of necessity embrace God as the Infinite Good, and not in the order of vision (the beatific vision), that a personal subject—a "someone"—can emerge in created being as a possible sharer in God's life in the beatific vision. In order to achieve God's purpose of sharing God's self with creatures so that they can participate in God's being and life, God must create spirits outside the vision of God in the order of grace, where they have free choice vis-à-vis God, so that through their free choice they can become persons who can share in God's life.

Human Suffering

The created spirit existing outside the beatific vision in the order of grace to become a person to whom God can give God's self in the beatific vision is capable of inflicting and undergoing destructive suffering. As we have seen, the created person, outside the vision of God, in its choices must proportion means to an end that is both other than and higher than itself, and so is capable of fault. The created person can inflict suffering on itself and/or others not only by its morally evil choice, but also by imperfect choices and errors.

Moreover, human beings, who become and define themselves as unique persons through multiple acts of free choice, must live outside the beatific vision for an extended time. In living outside the beatific vision, human beings are not united fully to the One they love. Hence, they experience this absence as desire. This state of separation and the resultant desire is a form of suffering. This is not simply a matter of the separation and estrangement of the sinner, but is part of what it means to be a human being. This living outside the beatific vision in a state of deep longing for God is the primordial suffering of the human being. It is not, however, of itself a destructive form of suffering.

The Suffering of the Human Person and Special Divine Action

In the analysis of God's freedom of exercise and freedom of specification, I argued that one cannot know why God permitted suffering in a particular instance or conversely whether God intervened (special divine action), unbeknown to the person, in other instances to prevent suffering. In light of the argument of this chapter, what the theologian can maintain is that God can neither create free creatures who by nature always act rightly nor can God create the creature and then immediately elevate the creature through the light of glory such that the creature would embrace God and be in the possession of its end (the beatific vision) through the first acts of its intellect and will. The creature, then, must initially live outside the beatific vision in the order of grace. In God's self-communication in the order of grace, God may act powerfully in the creature's life in such a way that the creature experiences itself as simply passive to the influence of God. There are many examples of this in the history of Christian spirituality. Let me quote Edith Stein in her description of her experience:

> There is a state of resting in God, an absolute break from all intellectual activity, when one forms no plans, makes no decisions and for the first time really ceases to act, when one simply hands over the future to God's will and "surrenders himself to fate." I myself have experienced this state to some extent. . . . [Resting in God] fills me with life. This invigorating flow of energy appears to be the result of an activity other than my own.[30]

While God may act powerfully in the creature's life in such a way that the creature experiences itself as simply passive to the influence of God, God's activity in this special mode cannot be continuous, like God's elevation of the creature in the beatific vision. Rather, in this life the created person must emerge through the created spirit's free choice. This is well attested in Christian life and practice. The initial conversion experience or heightened experiences of God's presence, when the creature experiences itself as passive to God's influence, are not continuous and give way to the ordinary working out of life where the creature must choose to continue to order itself to God as the object of its love. Edith Stein, for example, did not remain in this passive state; rather, she had to continue to choose God through her calling as a Carmelite nun.

While much more can and should be said about the problem of special divine action and human suffering, I suggest that the conclusion from the arguments of the first three parts of this essay sets the parameters for dealing with the theological issue of God's intervening in particular instances (special divine action) to prevent human suffering. In other words, however one works out a theology of special divine action in relation to human suffering, one must recognize that God's special divine action cannot be continuous, as in God's elevation of the creature in the beatific vision. Thus God cannot prevent destructive suffering in every instance or utterly alleviate the primordial suffering of human beings that result from them living outside union with God in the beatific vision.

Preserving the Mystery of God

While we have arrived at a very limited knowledge of the context within which God's freedom operates, such knowledge is crucial. It matters a great deal to know that God could not have achieved God's creative and salvific purpose without creatures' suffering. It is vitally important to know that God could not have achieved God's purpose by a simple divine fiat. It is essential to know that the suffering of human beings, and as such the eternal plan of providence and the unfolding of salvation history, including the Incarnation, are not simply the product of divine whim. It matters a great deal to know that the context within which "we live and move and have our being" (Acts 17:28) is not irrational and even absurd but is the mystery of God—a God who is drawing human persons to God's self so that they may experience the incomprehensible joy of sharing in God's life, but Who could not offer human persons the incomprehensible gift of union with God's self without the human person's and the human community's being subject to pain and suffering.

Notes

1. In David Hume, *Dialogues Concerning Natural Religion,* ed. Norman Kemp Smith, 2nd ed. (New York: T. Nelson, 1947), 198.

2. Archibald MacLeish, *J.B.; A Play in Verse* (Boston: Houghton Mifflin, 1958), 14.

3. Vatican I, *Dogmatic Constitution on the Catholic Faith*, chap. 4, in *The Christian Faith: In the Doctrinal Documents of the Catholic Church*, ed. Jacques Dupuis, SJ and J. Neuner, SJ, 6th ed. (New York: Alba House, 1996), 48.

4. The beatific vision refers to union with God in eternal life. It is beatific because it is the unsurpassable fulfillment of the human being. The ocular metaphor of vision is drawn from scripture (see, for example, 1 Cor 13:12; 1 Jn 3:2; Mt 5:8, 18:10; 2 Cor 5:7). Magisterial teaching holds that human beings see God immediately as God truly is (The Council of Florence, 1439) "with an intuitive vision and even face to face without the mediation of any creature by way of object of vision; . . . and in this vision they enjoy the divine essence" (Pope Benedict XII, *Benedictus Deus* 1336, in Dupuis and Neuner, *Christian Faith,* 943).

5. In Karl Rahner's thought, closeness to God does not erase the distinction; rather, closeness and autonomy increase in direct proportion. According to Rahner, "Because in the Incarnation the Logos creates the human reality by assuming it, and assumes it by emptying himself, for this reason there also applies here, and indeed in the most radical and specific and unique way, the axiom for understanding every relationship between God and creatures, namely, that closeness and distance, or being at God's disposal and being autonomous, do not vary for creatures in inverse, but rather in direct proportion. Christ is therefore man in the most radical way, and his humanity is the most autonomous and the most free not in spite of but because it has been assumed, because it has been created as God's self-expression." See Karl Rahner, *Foundations of Christian Faith: An Introduction to the Idea of Christianity*, trans. William V. Dych (New York: Crossroad, 1989), 226. This axiom from Rahner's Christology and theological anthropology informs his understanding of the beatific vision such that in the vision of God human beings experience the incomprehensibility and otherness of God most profoundly while simultaneously becoming radically irreducible selves. See also Karl Rahner, "Thomas Aquinas on the Incomprehensibility of God," in *Celebrating the Medieval Heritage: A Colloquy on the Thought of Aquinas and Bonaventure*, ed. David Tracy, *Journal of Religion* 58 (Supplement, 1978).

6. This runs all through Thomas Aquinas's thought, for example, *Summa theologiae* I.12.7; I.62.9; *Summa contra Gentiles* III.55. See also Gregory P. Rocca, OP, *Speaking the Incomprehensible God: Thomas Aquinas on the Interplay of Positive and Negative Theology* (Washington, DC: Catholic University of America, 2004), 36–48.

7. I have borrowed the language of "absolutely transcendental properties" and "transcendental relative properties" from Norris Clarke in order to describe Aquinas's treatment of attributes in terms of the transcendentals and in terms of the divine operation. See W. Norris Clarke, SJ, *The*

Philosophical Approach to God: A New Thomistic Perspective, 2nd rev. ed. (New York: Fordham University Press, 2007), 83–88.

8. See Thomas Aquinas *Summa theologiae* I. q. 14, introduction.

9. "At a minimum" refers to the fact that we do not fully know God's purpose. In addition, because we cannot know why God created a material universe, I want to indicate that my statement of God's purpose is minimalistic. I do not want to suggest that the materiality of the universe is secondary or unimportant, for Christianity believes in the resurrection of the body. About half the atoms in our bodies, including Jesus' body, come from the "big bang," so we are inextricably related to the whole of the universe. My point here is that we do not know why God created such a *material* universe.

10. All biblical quotations come from the New Revised Standard Version (NRSV).

11. When I speak of the possible (that is, intelligible) ways in which God's being and life can be communicated to creatures, this includes both the orders of creation and grace. In terms of creation, which includes conservation and governance, one is speaking of the limited ways in which God's being can be communicated. In the order of grace, one is maintaining that within the self-communication of God to all people in the mode of offer (Rahner's supernatural existential), the infinite God can touch a particular person in a particular way.

12. A human being cannot be united to God by its own act because God is beyond the natural powers of the finite human being. The human being is an *obediential potency* and as such the natural capacity of the human being can be elevated through God's free and gracious activity such that the human being can be united with God and can know God as God is.

13. When I use the terms *created spirit, free creature,* or *created person* I am referring to characteristics that are applicable to both human beings and angels. When I use the terms *human being, human person,* or *angel* I am referring to what is unique to each one respectively.

14. See Thomas Aquinas, *Summa contra Gentiles* III.2.[8].

15. W. Norris Clarke, "Freedom as Value," in *Freedom and Value,* ed. Robert O. Johann (New York: Fordham University Press, 1976), 14.

16. William Harmless, ed., *Augustine in His Own Words* (Washington, DC: Catholic University of America Press, 2010), 3.

17. "Being presented with the Infinite Good" presupposes the light of glory or God elevating the creature into the beatific vision. As we have seen, a creature cannot be united to God by his or her own act

because God is beyond the natural powers of the human being. The light of glory is an ontological determination of the knower that disposes the person to receive the vision. This determination is the effect of the self-communication of God in the person's interiority. If the ontological communication of God to the creature is the condition of the possibility of the beatific vision, then God is the giver of the gift of vision, the giving of the gift, and the gift itself. See Karl Rahner, "Some Implications of the Scholastic Concept of Uncreated Grace," in *Theological Investigations I: God, Christ, Mary, and Grace*, trans. Cornelius Ernst, OP (New York: Crossroad, 1982), 333.

18. Clarke, "Freedom as Value," 15.

19. Ibid.

20. Ibid., 16.

21. Carl W. Grindel, "Freedom of Autonomy—The Terminal Freedom," in *Concept of Freedom*, ed. Carl W. Grindel (Chicago: H. Regnery Co, 1955), 57.

22. Clarke, "Freedom as Value," 15.

23. A wrong action is an action that is either sinful or immoral or an error and is capable of being a source of destructive suffering. Conversely, a right action is an action that is neither sinful nor immoral nor an error and is incapable of being a source of destructive suffering. The issue here is not the moral analysis of an act but its capacity to inflict suffering.

24. In terms of the question of sin, sin is a religious concept indicating that in order to do evil, persons have to turn away from the influence of God's love in their life.

25. Thomas Aquinas, *Summa theologiae,* I.63.1. All translations of Aquinas are mine.

26. Ibid.

27. Ibid.

28. W. Norris Clarke*, Person and Being* (Milwaukee, WI: Marquette University Press, 1993), 29. The brackets in this instance are part of the quotation.

29. See ibid., 27.

30. In Waltraud Herbstrith, *Edith Stein: A Biography*, trans. Fr. Bernard Bonowitz, OCSO (San Francisco: Ignatius Press, 1992), 60.

FIVE

The Suffering of Christ

Michael J. Himes

Suffering and Creatureliness

My reflection on this profound and solemn subject is in three parts. The first and briefest asks the question, what do we mean by the word *suffering?* Clearly it does not simply mean pain, because there are many kinds of pain that we do not regard as suffering. For example, think of an athlete in rigorous training. He or she may experience intense physical pain, perhaps as intense as that felt by someone who is very ill. What is the difference? Why in the latter case do we describe the pain as suffering whereas in the former case we usually do not and, I suspect, the athlete would not? Why is pain sometimes regarded as suffering and sometimes not? What is the additional factor that makes some pain suffering? I suggest that it is our sense of lack of control. We speak of suffering when our experience of pain is not in our control, when we do not choose it, do not understand its purpose, and cannot see any good that can result from it. The essence of suffering is a sense of things being out of our control. We are not in charge of the pain. It does not "make sense" to us. We cannot use it for our own purposes. If this beyond-our-control experience is what makes pain into suffering, then suffering is very closely related to the experience of creatureliness, the recognition of being creature, of being finite, of being utterly dependent, of not causing ourselves to be.

The fragility, the "iffiness" of our existence is the always present though often unacknowledged background to everything we think or do. I cannot guarantee that I will be alive to finish this sentence that I am writing, nor can you be absolutely certain that you will survive to finish reading it. I have every good hope that I will still be alive when I finish this reflection on Christ's suffering, and I certainly hope that you will still be breathing when you are done reading it. But neither of us can *guarantee* it. We are not ultimately in control of our own existence. That is what it is to be a creature, and the reaction to the discovery of our creatureliness is all too often horror, anger, rebellion, and despair.

Genesis 3 is one of the wisest and most familiar stories ever written. It is, of course, the tale of the fall of Adam and Eve and the consequent loss of the garden of paradise. It is certainly a well-told story: it is over three thousand years old, has only four characters—God, the man, the woman, and the snake—and once one hears it one does not forget it. But it is not only well told, it is profoundly wise. Because the story is so familiar, I need only recall what I consider the central point of the passage. It is a story about how evil enters the world. The first two chapters of the Book of Genesis as it has stood for so many centuries tells us that God has created everything and that everything is good. Over and over again in the first chapter we are told that God looked at what he had made and saw that it was good (Gn 1:4, 10, 12, 18, 21, 25, and 31). But the two claims most insistently advanced by Genesis 1—that God is the creator of all that exists and that all that exists is good—present a problem that was as obvious to the tellers and hearers of this story thirty centuries ago as it is to us: if God is the origin and maker of everything that exists, and everything that God makes is good, how does it happen that evil exists? Where does evil come from?

The answer to that enormous question is found in chapter 3 and is one of the greatest insights of the Jewish and Christian traditions. What does the serpent say to the first man and woman that leads them into disobedience to God? What is the first temptation, according to Genesis 3? "Eat this, and then you will be like God." The temptation is not an invitation to disobedience, nor is it an appeal to pride. The fall of the first man and woman, according to Genesis 3, is due to their inability to believe that they really *are* like God. As the biblical text now stands and has stood for three millennia, the first thing we learn about being a human being is that we are created in God's likeness. Through the first five days of creation we are told that God looked at what he had created and saw that it was good—until the afternoon of the sixth day. (Presumably, God like a good orthodox Jew, rests on the Sabbath, so the whole of creation has to be completed on Friday before sunset.) At the conclusion of all his work, God now creates his masterpiece, and for the first time the now familiar pattern breaks. Previously God creates simply by speaking: God *said*, "Let there be X," and there was X, and God looked at it and saw that it was good. Now, however, God does not merely speak his creative word; now the text depicts God as deliberating and making a plan or model for this last creature. God has, as it were, a blueprint for the human being. The blueprint is God's self: "Let us make the human being in our image, in the likeness of ourselves" (Gn 3:26). The climax of the first chapter's account of creation is its insistence that God has made us in God's image and likeness, that being a human being *of its very nature* is to be *like* God. And two chapters later, the first man and woman face the first temptation, which is, in effect, not to believe chapter 1. Being human is not being like God! Being human is a mess. I do not control my own life. I cannot guarantee my own destiny. I cannot decide my own fate. I do not govern every aspect of my life. I am not omnipotent. I am not like God! To be like God I must do something, must seize control, must create myself. Being in God's image and likeness is not a gift given me by God; it is an achievement, an accomplishment. It is my work. How to start? Start by eating the fruit you have been told not to eat. We are all tempted to make ourselves like God, because what we are at the moment is not very wonderful.

As a matter of fact, what we are at the moment is a source of great anxiety. We are creatures: we are not in ultimate control, we are not the ultimate source of our existence, we are not the ultimate goal of our existence, we are not the ultimate meaning-givers of our own existence, and we are not the ultimate judges of the value of our own existence. And the response to that recognition is very often terror. Most of the time we hide it from ourselves. We occupy ourselves with making all sorts of small decisions or perhaps even large decisions and so think of ourselves as being in control of ourselves. But every now and again something happens that reminds us of the "iffiness" of our existence, its radical contingency, and our absolute dependence. The response may be rebellion, or resentment, or anger, or fear. It may be stronger than mere fear, it may be terror, and at its absolute worst it is despair.

Despair is the rejection of what we are because we are not God. It is the refusal to accept the goodness of being a creature. After all, we know God's judgment on creatures. Genesis 1 repeats and repeats that God looked at creatures and saw that they are good. Indeed, with the creation of the first human being in the Genesis 1 creation story, the adjective becomes stronger: God sees that creation is "very good." The temptation is to reject the truth of God's first judgment. God sees that all creation is good, but we agree with the serpent and reject the divine judgment precisely because we see creatures—including preeminently ourselves—as not good precisely because we are creatures. The reason why we refuse to believe in the goodness of creatureliness is that we are not fully in control. If the essence of suffering is our realization that we are not the origin, the end, or the controlling power of our existence, if suffering is finally our confrontation with our being creatures—if, therefore, we are unable to find or give meaning to our own pain and, perhaps more devastatingly, the pain of people we love, how are we to talk about Jesus' suffering.

Jesus' Suffering

I find it very interesting (and perhaps cautionary) that as we look back over the centuries to the disputes among Christians of the first and second centuries about who Jesus is and how he is to be thought about and spoken of and what his mission is, the earliest christological disputes and especially the rejected opinions (heresies, as we would now describe them) never deny or even question that Jesus is God. It seems that few people in antiquity had difficulty in accepting Jesus' divinity. The problem seems to have been that many people could not accept that he was really human. Most people today find little difficulty affirming that Jesus is fully human; the contemporary problem is that we are not sure that we know what it means to say he is fully divine. It is an extraordinary claim, that the one who is in the form of God (Phil 2:6), the eternal Son, the eternal Word, the eternal Logos of God, is fully human, as you and I are human, in all things except sin. For that means that he can be tempted. In his humanity he can be confronted with the possibility of despair, cannot see the meaning in his own suffering, cannot grasp what the will of the Father could possibly be for him. We might be able to imagine the Son of God becoming vulnerable enough to suffer physical pain, but to suffer mental anguish? To be genuinely terrified of the future? Not to know what his Father's plan is? Not to see how his mission accomplishes that plan? That is astonishing. How can that possibly be? And yet that is precisely what the Christian tradition insists is true about Jesus. Let me cite two examples.

I think that the crucial test for any Christology is whether it accords full weight to Jesus' agony in Gethsemane. If one thinks of the agony in the garden as merely a powerful and striking teaching device to impress a point on the disciples, if we treat the gospel account as a story of Jesus' *appearing* to be frightened, *seeming* to be worried, but in fact in full and perfect control of his situation—if we think that on Good Friday Jesus has a clear vision of Easter Sunday—then our Christology is deeply flawed. We must take Jesus' agony in the garden with full seriousness. Jesus is terrified. He is at a loss as to why the Father wills his death by torture. He experiences profound fear and deep loss. Far more than the physical pain that he is about to undergo, his agonized prayer is his plea to the Father that the seemingly utter failure of his mission makes no sense to him, that his life appears to have been pointless, that his death will have no meaning. This is real agony, suffering as the meaninglessness of creatureliness. It is in confronting this suffering that Jesus prays that his Father's will be accomplished even though it makes no sense to him at that moment.

Underscoring this point is another story that at first glance does not seem to have anything to do with the account of Jesus' agony in Gethsemane. The Gospel of John has no "agony in the garden" scene, nothing of the dramatic description of Jesus' prayer the night before his death that we find in Matthew's, Mark's, and Luke's Gospels (Mt 26: 36–46; Mk 14:32–42; Lk 22:39–46). There is a passage in John's Gospel, however, that I think is the Johannine equivalent to the agony in the garden in the Synoptic Gospels. It may not immediately appear to have much in common with the Gethsemane accounts, but I suggest that the story of the raising of Lazarus (Jn 11:1–44) is a parallel to them. Lazarus is an utterly unimportant character in that story. John's Gospel has no interest whatsoever in his experience either of dying or of being brought back to life. In fact, he does not speak a single syllable in the story. The passage is about Jesus and Jesus' response to what happened to his friend Lazarus. Notice that this story is the first time in the Fourth Gospel that Jesus confronts the deep creaturely reality of death. Until this point in John's Gospel, unlike the Synoptic Gospels, we find no mention of John the Baptist's death, or the raising of Jairus's daughter, or the restoration of the son of the widow of Naim. In fact, in the Fourth Gospel Jesus never directly encounters death until he learns of Lazarus's death. But is it really Lazarus's death that he meets? When Martha and Mary bring him to their brother's tomb, it is described as "a cave sealed by a stone." This might be a general description of many burials in ancient Palestine, but surely it was meant to strike the reader or hearer of the account as reminiscent of the burial place of Jesus. It is not only his friend Lazarus's tomb to which Jesus is led by the mourners; it is "the Tomb"—his, yours, mine, and Lazarus's. Jesus meets not only Lazarus's death but his own, which will come so quickly. In the Gospels of Matthew and Mark, Jesus prays three times with anguished emotion. In John's story of the raising of Lazarus, three times Jesus is described as deeply troubled and profoundly moved even to the point of tears (Jn 11:32, 35, and 38). It is striking that, before he arrives in Bethany, where Lazarus and his sisters Martha and Mary reside, Jesus seems calm and serenely assured that no harm will come to his friend. That changes dramatically when he is met by the mourners and both Martha and Mary say that, had he been present, their brother would not have died. The sisters are convinced that Jesus is in control. Had he arrived earlier, he could have prevented Lazarus's death. Indeed, Martha is sure that Jesus can still make all right again: "Even now I know that God will grant whatever you ask of him" (Jn 11:22). In effect, they say to Jesus, "Finally you are able to eliminate pain and suffering. Everything is within your power; nothing is beyond your control. All things are subject to you." And yet, Jesus is deeply upset and weeps at the tomb. He prays to his Father: "Father, I thank you for hearing my prayer. I know that you always hear me." But there will come a time, although not in the Fourth Gospel, that Jesus will pray in the depth of his agony, and his Father seems to remain silent. In both prayers, that at Lazarus's tomb and that in Gethsemane, Jesus says to the Father: "Ultimately this is your will, Father. Let my will be whatever your will is." That is the key. In the face of his hideous death he does not claim to be in control.[1]

If Jesus were in control, that is, if he did not suffer as he faced the terror of death, then those early heretical Christologies would be correct. Those docetic understandings of Jesus' person and work insisted that he could not be really and fully human.[2] His apparent humanity was an illusion. The Son does an excellent impersonation of a human being, but finally that is all that it is—an impersonation. The Son of God can disguise himself as a human being very effectively, but he is not human as all other human beings are human. He is not really like us in all things except sin (Heb 4:15).

The issue, however, is not sin; it is fear, terror, utter bewilderment. It is the experience of being at a loss, the sense of not being in control. It is a question of suffering. If we do not see that in Jesus, then we do not see Jesus, because we do not really believe in the incarnation. Jesus really suffers with us, but the suffering is not only pain, not only the physical horror of crucifixion. It is the anguish of not seeing where we are going, of not controlling our destiny, of being swept along helplessly, of losing ourselves.

This leads us inevitably to the question of how we are saved by Jesus' suffering. The Christian tradition does not simply affirm that Jesus suffers with us. It maintains that because he suffers with us, everything is changed. So we must ask now, how are we different? How are we saved by the fact that Jesus has suffered?

Jesus' Suffering and Our Salvation

Certainly we are not saved because Jesus' suffering pleases an overly demanding parent. Jesus does not suffer to assuage the anger of the Father. Nor is his suffering a matter of paying the penalty demanded by God's justice. The first makes God into a monster, and the latter seems to imply that justice is an abstract requirement above God that God must fulfill. How does Jesus' suffering change us? The image we find in the Gospels is that we take up our crosses and follow Jesus (Mt 16:24; Mk 8:34; Lk 9:23). Jesus establishes the pattern that discloses the true shape of our existence. This is not salvation by education. Jesus is not only a teacher giving his followers instructions about how they are to live. He does not teach us what we are to do; rather, he reveals how things have always been. He does not tell us what to do; he shows us what human existence is. By living our humanity as he has lived his humanity we are saved.

How does Jesus live his humanity? In Gethsemane the Father's will is a dark and profound mystery to him. What is his response to the mystery of the Father's will? How does Jesus respond to the fact of his creatureliness, his not being in control of his destiny, his suffering? He says yes to it. His yes, however, is not a simple surrender, not the easy yes of fatalism or a stoic bearing up under the burden. It is not the easy yes of a seemingly religious quiet-ism. It is a struggle. Jesus in Gethsemane does not quietly accept the Father's will. He struggles to the conclusion: "Not my will but yours be done."

This struggle with God is illustrated in one of the most power-ful and moving images in the Hebrew scriptures (again found in Genesis). It is the mysterious event that occurs the night before Jacob returns to Canaan. Years earlier he had cheated his brother,

Esau, out of his birthright. Now he is returning home with two wives and a number of sons, a household of servants and dependents, and all his flocks. He has pitched camp on the bank of a river and plans to cross into the Promised Land the next morning. He is understandably anxious about what may await him and his family, not least Esau, his cheated brother, who, as far as Jacob knows, is still furious about the way his younger twin had deceived him so many years before. That night Jacob cannot sleep. As he walks along the river bank, someone seizes him and begins to wrestle with him in the dark. And they wrestle all night, he and this mysterious figure whom Jacob recognizes to be a supernatural presence. As the dawn breaks, his opponent commands Jacob to release him and gives him a blow that dislocates his hip. Jacob refuses to let his mysterious assailant go until his attacker blesses him. The angel, the presence of God, does so. He also changes Jacob's name, always a matter of great significance in the scriptures. Henceforward, he tells Jacob, he will be called Israel, which the text interprets for us as "he who struggles with God." And so the angel of God blesses him and departs, and Jacob continues across the river with his family, limping as he goes (Gn 32:23–33).

Enigmatic as it is, this story is a startlingly accurate image of God's relationship with both Israel and the church, the New Israel. The name given to God's people, whether of the first covenant or of the second, is Israel, the one who struggles with God. The people of God, both the Old and the New Israel, are not designated as those who obey God or heed God or love God or are faithful to God. We are the people who struggle with God. God's people are those who wrestle with God all through the darkness of the night and who at dawn enter the Promise Land but only enter it limping. God's people are those whom God has crippled. To wrestle with God is to accept suffering. To take up one's cross and follow Jesus is not passive resignation to the will of God. It is a struggle with God so fierce that, when the night is past and the sun rises, we can ask for God's blessing and limp toward the kingdom to which God has called us. Like the risen Christ, we carry the scars of our struggle with God. Like Jacob struggling through the night with the angel on the river bank, Jesus struggles with the Father's mysterious will in the darkness in Gethsemane. This is what it means to shoulder our cross and follow Jesus. We must bear the scars of our suffering as Jesus displays the wounds of his suffering even after he has been raised. One cannot enter the kingdom of God unscathed. Jesus' experience is the pattern of our experience. We finally say yes to God's will, even though we do not see its point or its meaning or its purpose.

There is a popular misunderstanding of theology that is destructive of faith. Often it is thought, not least by theologians, that the theological task is to provide persuasive answers to religious questions. It is not. Theology's task is to clarify exactly how difficult, how puzzling, and how pressing the questions are. Far from resolving the problems believers encounter, the theological task is to lead believers to see the full weight of those problems. Theology forces us to confront just how difficult it is to believe. Theology is at its most distorted when it convinces us that all the pieces of our experience fit together, that all the puzzles are solved, that all the answers have been given, in short, when it does away with suffering. Faith that assures us that following Jesus means taking up a cross of precisely the right weight and walking a perfectly straight road is false faith. Religious belief that confidently tells us that we need not suffer in our own personal Gethsemane ends by deluding us into thinking that we need not watch and pray all night but can instead go to sleep in the garden like the disciples. True faith demands that we see and feel how immensely deep and how darkly mysterious the experience of being a human being is and to know what a fearful thing it is to be creature before the Creator. Religious belief does not take away suffering or make it easier.

Faith enables us to hold with equal strength the reality of our suffering and the conviction that God's will is always love. When Jesus prays that the Father's will be done, what he prays is that God will love. God does not will a multiplicity of things. God wills one thing and one thing only—love, *agape*, self-gift. It may well happen that at any particular moment I cannot understand how my pain and suffering fit with that perfect love. As a believer my calling is not to surrender either pole of my experience, not to deny either God's love or my suffering. I must neither convince myself that the pain is an illusion and that, as a believer, I must "rise above it" nor dismiss the perfect self-giving love of God as a delusion. Following the pattern of Jesus, I must hold on to both as true. To embody the pattern of Jesus, to take up our cross and follow him, we must remain faithful both to the reality of suffering and to the absolute love of God and not surrender either one to the other.

The most poignant suffering, I find, is watching someone we love suffer and not being able to do anything to alleviate it. We would gladly do whatever is required to end the suffering. We would joyfully take up the suffering of the loved one and bear it ourselves. But we cannot. In the face of that helplessness, to affirm with equal strength that God is love and that witnessing the pain of those we love is unbearable is to share the suffering of Jesus in Gethsemane. Not to be able to see how those two truths are reconcilable is to discover the awesome depth of the word that we religious believers often use so lightly: *mystery.* The alternative to living in and with the mystery of creatureliness is despair. I know of no more accurate statement of what it means to live faithfully in and with this mystery than that given by Gerard Manley Hopkins in one of his last sonnets:

> Not, I'll not, carrion comfort, Despair, not feast
>   on thee;
> Not untwist—slack they may be—these last
>   strands of man
> In me or, most weary, cry *I can no more.* I can;
> Can something, hope, wish day come, not choose
>   not to be.[3]

There are times when the only thing one can do is at least not choose not to be. Indeed, that may be the most sacred task we are given. God has called us into being and pronounced our being good. The opposite is to reject the goodness of our finite being and choose nonbeing. To be, even at the cost of suffering, is to reject despair. At least—and perhaps, at most—we can "not choose not to be."

To refuse the "carrion comfort" of despair requires us to discover the presence of God in diminishment as well as growth. I know what it is like to experience the presence of God as one grows and learns and meets dear and deeply loved friends. I know what it feels like to see life spread out before one and find an abundance of opportunities open. I know how to see God in growth and expansion. All of us do. But all of us have to learn to see God in diminishment, to celebrate God's presence as things close down around us, as horizons narrow and possibilities grow fewer. To see not the birth of new life but the passing of old, familiar, and terribly dear lives—to find God in the weary end and no longer in the promising beginning—that is what I need to learn now. Having quoted one great poet, let me cite another. As I grow older, the closing lines of T. S. Eliot's "East Coker," the second of his *Four Quartets*, have come to mean a great deal to me. Using the image of a voyage on the cold waters of the polar sea, he wrote:

> Old men ought to be explorers
> Here and there does not matter
> We must be still and still moving
> Into another intensity
> For a further union, a deeper communion
> Through the dark cold and the empty desolation,
> The wave cry, the wind cry, the vast waters
> Of the petrel and the porpoise. In my end is my
>   beginning.[4]

Old people, and all of us get older every day, ought to be explorers. There is new and unexplored territory before us—unexplored, at least, by me. I know what it is like to grow, now I must learn what it is like to fade. I know what it is like to be born, now I must find out what it is like to die. Such exploration requires remaining still, as Eliot wrote, because it is a matter not of going out but of going in—moving into that vast desolation, the vast, cold waters of the petrel and the porpoise. But when we set sail, our end is our beginning. We learned that long ago on the banks of the Jordan and in the garden of Gethsemane.

Notes

1. It should be noted that the Gospel of John seems so intent on asserting the divine power and majesty in Jesus that it not only omits any mention of the Synoptics' Gethsemane scene, it seems to explicitly reject any suffering (in the way I have described it here) in Jesus' experience. At the moment of his arrest (Jn 18:4–9) Jesus demonstrates that he is in full and perfect control of the situation. But in John 12:27 we find that, as the time of his Passover draws near, he is again described as deeply troubled, and he prays that the Father's will be done, adding that he will not ask the Father to save him from "this hour" (although that is precisely what he does pray in the Synoptic Gospels), for this hour is the reason that he has come into the world.

2. The term *docetic* (from the Greek verb *dokein*, meaning "to seem" or "to appear") has traditionally been used to describe various primitive attempts to describe Jesus as a manifestation of God in our world in the semblance or under the appearance of a human person. Many such early attempts denied the physical reality of Jesus' body and so denied that he truly died.

3. Gerard Manley Hopkins, *The Poems of Gerard Manley Hopkins,* 4th ed., ed. W. H. Gardner and N. H. MacKenzie (London: Oxford University Press, 1967), 99.

4. T. S. Eliot, *Collected Poems, 1909–1962* (New York: Harcourt, Brace, and World, 1963), 189–90.

SIX

Suffering in Christian Life and Experience

Elizabeth A. Dreyer

When I was invited to address the topic of suffering and Christian discipleship in thirty minutes, I gasped. When I accepted the invitation, I knew that I could count myself among fools who enter where angels fear to tread! I began to wonder what others might include in such an address, so I polled a few friends and family members who live and think deeply. Two women in mid-life wrote that they had not suffered anything serious enough to merit inclusion. Others were able to identify very specific painful events in their lives. Still others shared thoughts, metaphors, and insights.

An octogenarian artist friend of mine, whose wisdom seems boundless, recommended that I check what I had already written about suffering in my book, Earth Crammed with Heaven *(even mentioning specific page numbers!). But her second suggestion captured my attention. She wrote: "Maybe the lecturer should simply walk to the podium, stand and weep for thirty minutes, inviting the audience to weep with her." She was right. Such an act would be better than a thousand words. This idea emerged from an experience she had had of a workshop on joy. "The speaker played audio tapes of persons laughing. He started laughing himself. Soon we were all engaged in hearty belly laughs!"*

127

This chapter is the presentation that resulted. I don't ask that we literally spend thirty minutes weeping, but my first "word" about suffering is a plea to allow ourselves to express our sadness about our broken hearts and the suffering of the world.

Personal Context

I began work on this presentation during Holy Week: the liturgy of Palm Sunday, Maundy Thursday, Good Friday, and the Easter Vigil. I also attended a concert, "Music for Palm Sunday," performed by the Yale Camerata and orchestra, the Elm City Girls' Choir, four soloists (one in his forties) and three fifth-graders from a local boys choir. They performed David Lang's *Little Match Girl Passion,* for which Lang was awarded the Pulitzer Prize for music in 2008. The story is based on Hans Christian Andersen's story of the same name, first published in 1845.

Tim Page, a Pulitzer juror and *Washington Post* music critic, wrote of this music: "I don't think I've ever been so moved by a new, and largely unheralded, composition as I was by David Lang's *Little Match Girl Passion*, which is unlike any music I know."[1] In the program notes the composer wrote: "What has always interested me is that Andersen tells this story as a kind of parable, drawing a religious and moral equivalency between the suffering of the poor girl and the suffering of Jesus. The girl suffers, is scorned by the crowd, dies and is transfigured." While Lang recasts the tale in the format of Bach's *St. Matthew Passion*, he maintains that there is no Bach in the piece and no Jesus—"rather the suffering of the Little Match Girl has been substituted for Jesus's, elevating (I hope) her sorrow to a higher plane."[2]

I cite one section of the libretto that functioned as the *Kyrie* of the piece.

> Have mercy, my God
> Look here, my God.
> See my tears fall. See my tears fall.
> Have mercy, my God. Have mercy.

My eyes are crying.
My heart is crying, my God.
See my tears fall.
See my tears fall, my God.[3]

In late May, I traveled through Eastern Europe from Vienna, Austria, to Bucharest, Romania. It was a challenge to hold in tension the beauty of the Danube and its history of war and violence suffered for millennia. We were in Belgrade the day Ratko Mladić was arrested—reminding all of the ravages of the Bosnian war. We were told that in the last two thousand years, Belgrade had been razed forty times. I thought once again, who am I to speak of suffering?

Global Context

Suffering is a staple of life, a part of what it means to be a human being. In the end we don't have much control over it, although our "medicalized culture of comfort" in the developed world works heroically to convince us otherwise. Contrast the rhetoric of the "golden years" to the relentless journey toward aging, illness, and death.[4] The last century witnessed catastrophic suffering—"the Turkish massacre of the Armenians, the Nazi Holocaust, the Soviet purges, the Japanese rape of Nanking, the American atomic destruction of Hiroshima, the Chinese Great Cultural Revolution, Cambodian killing fields, and the Rwandan genocide."[5] We hear daily of the escalating Palestinian-Israeli conflict; wars in Iraq and Afghanistan; upheaval in Egypt, Syria, Tunisia, Bahrain, and Libya; poverty, famine, displacement, and illness of millions of people.

The inevitable suffering in life, horrendous historical suffering, and present global suffering are filtered through the lens of our present North American circumstances and often mark our experience of suffering in three ways. First, our constant exposure to violence makes it more difficult to develop empathy in the face of human misery. In addition, the comfortable circumstances in which most of us live have raised our expectations that a "quick fix" should be available for our suffering.[6] American advertising bombards us with information about drugs, creams, defoliants, anti-fungals, stimulants, relaxers, gels, prophylactics to alleviate even our most minor discomforts. Science and money have made it easier to ease pain, multiply creature comforts, enhance health, and postpone death.[7] Healing is good and desirable as long as we don't view the world's misery as unrelated to us, but rather the lot of others from which we are exempt.

Second, the telecommunications revolution heightens our awareness of suffering. The evening news places before us each day the faces of war, starvation, and disease on every continent. We are no longer ignorant of the plight of peoples in far-flung locations—suffering that in an earlier age we would not have known existed. Paradoxically, such exposure can make us numb, reducing our ability to enter compassionately into the lives of the "crucified" among us.

Third, we live in an era of significant growth in interfaith dialogue. The meaning of suffering is an integral part of all world religions. Throughout history, faith communities have pondered the meaning of suffering and its relationship to evil. Buddhists, Jews, Sikhs, Muslims, Hindus, and Christians have different stories to tell and various creative, yet imperfect, responses to human suffering. In order to survive into the future, we have to become more knowledgeable not only about our own traditions, but also about those of others. Through listening to one another with an open ear and empathetic heart, we can learn to name better the strengths and weaknesses of our own traditions. Author James Fredericks notes how interreligious friendships "help us to resist the multiple strategies we have for domesticating demanding truths or inoculating ourselves from their transformative power."[8] But here I begin at home, reflecting on suffering in the light of the Christian tradition.

Types of Suffering

It is important to distinguish among various kinds of suffering, the causes of suffering, the different ways the immediacy of suffering informs our experience of suffering, the depth of our suffering, and possible responses to suffering.

Kinds and Causes of Suffering

There are various kinds of suffering: bodily, mental, emotional, psychological, and spiritual. And there are various causes of suffering—disasters of nature, accidents, human agency, or illness. Some take on suffering because of altruism or love. Others suffer from ignorance, or physical or psychological dysfunction. There is suffering that is accidentally caused, and suffering deliberately and maliciously inflicted.

In addition to the causes, types and responses to suffering, we can distinguish between suffering that we choose and suffering that "happens" to us. Ascetic practices such as fasting and keeping vigil in prayer have long been revered in the Christian tradition. There are also more dramatic forms of chosen suffering: donating an organ, taking someone's place in prison, putting oneself at risk to save another, responding affirmatively to live out a prophetic call. Other suffering is chosen indirectly when we choose to risk ourselves in love and suffer the consequences. In 1944, from Berlin's Tegel Prison, Dietrich Bonhoeffer wrote: "We are summoned to share in God's suffering at the hands of a godless world."[9]

Then there is the suffering that comes to us. I remember the words of another wise friend: "If you live with your eyes open, you never have to go to Lent. Lent always comes to you." While I have nothing against giving up chocolate, saying an extra prayer, or serving at a food kitchen during Lent, the real challenge involves suffering that comes as part of our daily lives: unemployment; losing a home; violence; the cruel word; addiction; illness; intractably malfunctioning relationships; the utter stupidity of aspects of daily life; the breakdown of sight, hearing, joints, and mental abilities in old age.

Nature also deals harsh blows, suffering that we problematically call acts of God. The images of the earthquake and tsunami in Japan in March 2011 and the more recent flooding and forest fires in the United States remain vivid in our minds.

What we say about one type of suffering may be totally false when applied to another. The result of getting things mixed up has, and will continue to produce, unnecessary suffering. For example, suffering wrongly attributed to God can result in painful conflicts about belief. In other cases, false guilt can deaden a person's spirit and creative life.

The Immediacy of Suffering

Suffering should be further distinguished between suffering close to home and the suffering of those geographically removed from us. Personal suffering gets our attention quickly and is felt quite differently from the pain we might experience because of the suffering of people in Iraq or Afghanistan. Our response to these types of suffering is also likely to be quite different.

The Depth of Suffering

While it is impossible to determine the "more" or "less" of suffering in individual cases, it is important to recognize that there are differences in the depth of suffering. Here I distinguish four broad categories of suffering. The first is suffering that causes minor inconveniences: a scrape on the knee, a fender bender, a friend who forgets a birthday, a rejection letter from a publisher for a short story. A second type of suffering is more severe: hip replacement surgery, loss of a friendship, contentiousness and quarrelling. A third form might involve the death of a loved one, losing a job, watching our home succumb to a flood, battling cancer or addiction. Finally, there is catastrophic suffering: torture, murder, genocide, systematic rape as a military strategy, enslavement. This last category of suffering is aimed at the total destruction of the human being, and none of our ordinary words about suffering apply to it. As Christian disciples we are called to attend to all forms of suffering. Even though most of us are not directly involved in the horrors of war, displacement, and torture, we must take account of such catastrophic suffering in our theologies and spiritualities.

We can also distinguish some general human responses to suffering: we can rebel and revolt and shake an angry fist at God (Ivan Karamazov; Camus's *Rebel*); we can hold God accountable, putting God on trial (Elie Wiesel); we can respond stoically, with a stiff upper lip; we can decide ultimately to place faith and trust in God (Job); we can grow in compassion and humility, reaching out with ever greater commitment to alleviate the sufferings of others (Mother Teresa).[10]

In the end it is intimidating, even impudent, to talk about suffering. How can we who are so comfortable speak of suffering without doing injustice to those who have experienced unspeakable catastrophe? How do we minimize the danger that our language about suffering will be removed from the concrete horrors experienced by our sisters and brothers across the world? Any discussion of suffering must exist concretely "on the ground" and in our guts as well as in our ideas and words about it. Reason and logic do not suffice.

Suffering is a universal part of human life—related not only to religion, spirituality, theology, and ministry, but also to science and medicine, economics, education, politics, and war. We attend to it in order to understand, enter into, bring comfort, and resist the causes of suffering in creative and dedicated ways. Words are not perfect. They can be way off the mark, and even the best of words about suffering *always* remain inadequate. But we need words for conversation, without which we cannot live generously and compassionately as the body of Christ.

With this map of some of the contexts and types of suffering, I offer seven themes related to suffering that seem to me to be particularly important and relevant to the present moment.

Theological Themes and the Problem of Suffering

Suffering in Itself Is Evil

Suffering, *in and of itself*, is evil. The cross is of value because it was the fruit of a life of unconditional love. Jesus no more wanted to die an agonizing death than Martin Luther King Jr. wanted to be assassinated. No one wants to go to the cross. Nevertheless, the cross comes. As Christians search for understanding and courage in suffering, they turn to the cross of Christ for meaning. We believe that death, in whatever form, is not the last word. Resurrection has happened. Faith in this story allows Christians to bear, endure, and even consecrate, personal or communal suffering.[11] Our trust that goodness and redemption can emerge from evil and suffering should not, however, confuse us about the evil of suffering. God does not wish or cause or impose suffering on creation. It would be a tragedy if this common misreading of the Christian story dulled our sensibilities to notice suffering, minimized our horror at its brutality, or lessened our will to alleviate it.

Christian explanations for suffering have been numerous, diverse, and uneven: it is the result of cosmic forces of good and evil battling it out (creation myths from many religions); suffering is retribution for personal and communal transgressions; it atones for sin and brings redemption (Anselm in the twelfth century); it takes the form of natural growing pains as the cosmos matures and develops; it is an inevitable consequence of human freedom; it is part of God's mysterious ways, and humans shouldn't ask too many questions about it (Job); it is an invitation to conversion; it is a test to make us strong; it is a means of purification; it teaches us important truths; innocent suffering will be rewarded and perpetrators punished in the final judgment (the Beatitudes and Matthew 25).

We need to tread carefully here. Too often, in our search for the meaning of suffering, we say things that are simply untrue and often harmful. Many religious people stand guilty of inflicting suffering on other human beings through facile talk—we too easily counsel people not to complain; to accept the status quo; to wait for a better day. One comment I often hear that seems subtly pernicious to me is this: "God is faithful, and he will not let you be tested beyond your strength" (see 1 Cor 10:13). African slaves were told by Christian pastors that their plight was the will of God.[12] Battered women are sent back to their violent husbands. Public religious voices preached the destruction of 9/11 as retribution for the behaviors of feminists, abortionists, pagans, gays and lesbians (for example, Jerry Falwell).

We have perpetuated masochism, guilt, depression, and paralysis in the face of the crying needs of the world. We have a tradition in which many saints subjected themselves to extreme fasting, sleep deprivation, and flagellation. While we need to situate these practices in their historical context, they have too often resulted in a tendency to ennoble, glorify, bless, and celebrate suffering. Victims of suffering have been encouraged to accept suffering passively or to "spiritualize" their suffering.

How we celebrate Jesus' suffering and death (and resurrection) makes a difference in peoples' lives and in the world. Therefore, it is imperative that we get it right. If suffering has meaning, that meaning is love, for it is love that motivates us to weep and gnash our teeth, to walk beside one another, to bandage one another's wounds, to fight for justice and the abolition of suffering.

Who Is God?: Theodicy

Reflection on suffering in Christian life and experience engages us in the long tradition in Western Christianity that asks: if God is all good and all powerful, then how can bad things happen? In particular we ask: how do bad things happen to good people?[13] In most of the world's religions, God and suffering are related: from the depths of the agonized cry—"How long, O Lord?" (Ps 13:1; 35:17; 79:5)[14]—to sophisticated biblical and theological reflection on God's identity and relationship to suffering and evil.[15] The Christian God has been assigned diverse roles when it comes to suffering.[16] Does God *cause* suffering? Does God *allow* suffering? Can God suffer and still remain God? If God can't fix things, then God is not all powerful. If God can fix things but does not, then God becomes a cold-hearted, indifferent deity—a God that some feel compelled to defend in the face of crushing poverty and dehumanization. The experience of intense and unfair suffering is a primary reason many believers abandon faith. But in the face of suffering, believers ask: to whom do we pray?

The image of a patriarchal war-god does not accurately reflect the person of Jesus. The stories we have about Jesus reveal a man of peace. He did not glorify suffering. He did not recommend suffering, although he did say that following him would bring suffering in its wake. He did not advocate a "quick fix" for suffering. He did not promise a world in which there would be no suffering, short of the in-breaking of the kingdom of God. He did not rationalize suffering. His entrance into history did not change the fact of suffering. Suffering remains one of the great irrationalities of human existence.[17]

German theologian Johann Baptist Metz criticizes theologies that do not take seriously the negativity of suffering, that excuse it, that trivialize it with explanation, or that succumb to the temptation to defend God. He invites us to question God passionately and relentlessly about the world's suffering—refusing to settle for a familiar theory about God or a tidy answer.[18] Are there alternatives to a God who reigns in imperial splendor? Does the fact of the crucifixion of Jesus alter the way we think about God—from One who is impassible to One who is filled with compassion? Judaism has something to teach us here about how God truly can be Lord of the universe and, at the same time, engaged, merciful, and compassionate. Some theologians prefer that we not talk about God in terms of power at all. But this approach presumes that power can be viewed only as unilateral or controlling and ignores other ways in which genuine power can be shared and life giving.

Among others, feminist and process theologians have been in the vanguard of this critique. Feminists approach traditional theologies of the cross with reserve, all too aware of the ways in which they have been used to oppress women.[19] Without a sense of self and authentic freedom, women have followed the counsel to suffer in silence at great cost to their dignity and well-being, not to mention detriment to the wider community. Power in weakness is not real power when it is exercised because of coercion, fear, low self-esteem, or the desire to please those in the dominant group who set the rules.[20]

Process theologians envision God as profoundly affected by our suffering. God is God *because* God embraces and absorbs *all the suffering in the world* in love and compassion. Process theology challenges thinking about the power of God in terms of might and empire and control. The God spawned by Constantine conflicts mightily with the God of Gethsemane and Golgotha. The process view—that God chooses not to hoard power but truly to share it with creation—invites reflection. We labor to link present experience with the tradition, searching for new and provocative language and concepts for God in the midst of a suffering world.[21]

The Call to Alleviate Suffering

Modernization and secularization have caused our spiritualities to become more this-worldly and practical. The Christian life demands that we act to prevent, remove, and heal suffering. The miracle stories reveal how Jesus dealt with individual suffering— the raising of Jairus's daughter and Lazarus; the healing of the woman with an issue of blood; the repair of the soldier's ear in the garden of suffering. We also witness Jesus' indignant response to pharisaic legalism that demanded that the woman who had been crippled for eighteen years wait one more day for a cure because it was the Sabbath (Lk 13:10–17). Jesus does not want the law to prolong suffering—even that of his disciples nibbling corn in the fields on the Sabbath because they were hungry. "Nothing drew more severe words from Jesus . . . than words and actions which bring suffering to others" or that showed indifference to it (Mt 18:32–34; 23:4).[22] In addition, in Matthew's Gospel the criteria upon which we will be judged involve bringing relief to those who are suffering—feeding the hungry, giving drink to the thirsty, offering hospitality to the stranger, visiting those in prison (25:31–46).

The letter to the Galatians records the following command: "Bear one another's burdens and in this way you will fulfill the law of Christ" (6:2). Paul describes this way of living as being "in Christ," that is, conforming our lives to Jesus' ways of self-giving love. In an article on human suffering Elise Saggau explores the nuances of Christian discipleship. She speaks of solidarity not as an artificial attempt to share the suffering of others, but as a movement into the depth of one's own life. Self-knowledge brings the realization that we are all connected, that individual suffering or joy affects the whole community. In its depths, Christian life cannot flourish when we stand apart from suffering or exist in splendid isolation in pseudo hope, health, and wealth. We are called to cross over and stand with others, affirming their human potential to make choices that are humanizing and even divinizing—even in the midst of suffering.[23] Just as Jesus transformed suffering *from within*, opening himself to the sorrow that comes from standing with those who suffer, so must we.

We have success stories—Dorothy Day, the founder of the Catholic Worker movement in New York City; Bishop Desmond Tutu of South Africa; Mother Teresa; our brothers and sisters in Central America who gave their lives in their nonviolent fight against suffering and evil—Oscar Romero, Maura Clarke, Dorothy Kazel, Ita Ford. But in addition to these very public stories are millions of private stories of people who work each day to prevent, alleviate, and heal suffering. I remember well the words of a religious sister who had spent a lifetime in justice work. For her, the sin against the Holy Spirit was to be aware of suffering and do nothing. We stand convicted.

Prophetic Utterance

It is hard to step out of line in the ways Jesus did—speaking the truth to power and suffering the consequences. Some in his milieu assigned the worst possible construction to his words and actions. At times, Jesus' harsh words—"whitened sepulchers" and "brood of vipers"—suggest that their criticism stung him deeply.[24]

Jesuit John Dear encourages us to practice a spirituality of nonviolent resistance.[25] He reminds us that in the Sermon on the Mount, Jesus warns against basing our nonviolent resistance in anger, as anger cannot sustain us for the long haul. Rather, Jesus advocates two specific emotions: grief and joy in solidarity with our suffering sisters and brothers.

The Holy Spirit's power provides insight and energy for prophetic witness. The Spirit casts out fear, enabling us to speak out against the forces that inflict suffering on the world. Christian discipleship involves examining our fears, and inviting the breath of the Spirit to blow through them.[26] The first disciples were transformed at Pentecost. Their timidity and isolation were transformed into Spirit power and courage to speak and act in the world. Of course, the more we have to lose, the harder it is to be free to speak and act on behalf of the crucified among us. But there is no doubt that this is the call of the Christian life.

Loss and Grief

Much suffering involves loss and grief. One woman wrote to me about her lost son, whom she gave up for adoption when she was eighteen. Another spoke of losing a father to alcoholism when she was eleven. The range of losses is as wide as the number of people on earth. Yet another lost a husband of forty years when he left her and five children in the midst of a life crisis. Many in our society have lost jobs, homes, and life savings. We lose children to illness and addictions. The one Catholic priest I consulted mentioned the terrible loss to the church caused by limiting women's gifts.

Another metaphor for severe suffering is imprisonment, what Baltimore Carmelite Connie Fitzgerald calls impasse. We become trapped in difficult, demeaning, life-draining situations. Everything has been tried, and nothing works. Even when support is available—which is not always the case—persons in such darkness cannot receive it. These dark nights jolt and threaten us. Fitzgerald turns to the writings of John of the Cross to chart a way into the depths of powerlessness. This involves trusting that in the very darkness, God is working to open the way to new, intuitive, imaginative solutions. Instead of being the enemy, the darkness beckons to contemplation, to a new openness to the dark mystery of God, as we turn ourselves over in trust to the Holy Spirit.[27]

The United States is about to embark on a massive demographic change as "baby boomers" become sixty-five. The census in 2000 counted 79.6 million US residents born in the years 1946 through 1964. No doubt we will witness an abundance of fiction, poetry, art, film, and spiritualities about aging and death: Dolores Leckey's

Grieving with Grace; Joan Didion's *The Year of Magical Thinking;* Meghan O'Rourke's *The Long Goodbye;* Antonia Fraser's *Must You Go? My Life with Harold Pinter;* Christopher Reid's *A Scattering.* In a review of O'Rourke's book, Gail Caldwell writes: "Grief doesn't necessarily make you noble. Sometimes it just makes you crazy, or primitive with fear." O'Rourke writes of not being prepared for the "physical goneness of her mother, or for the dearth of ritual and understanding that would acknowledge her loss."[28] The Christian story and the rituals of the church provide a rich heritage that can accompany us through the suffering of loss and death. They do not work for everyone or in all times and situations, but for many, ritual can be laid as a palimpsest over our lives of suffering, loss, death, and grief—providing meaning, solace, even joy.

There is something infinitely personal and yet universal about loss and grief. Reflection on these experiences can be broad and deep and go beyond our repulsion or fascination with death. What will come forth from this massive baby-boomer population who now begin the journey of aging and entertain the prospect of death from a closer vantage point? How will the experience of this large group of Americans affect our death-denying culture that craves, and spends billions on, the dream of eternal youth?

A neighbor speaks of the "aching and enduring sense of loss" she feels as her husband, who suffers from Parkinson's disease, loses his ability to move or control his muscles—the lynchpin of communication. She noted that 70–90 percent of what we communicate to one another—at any time—is nonverbal. I hear often from those who make it to eighty years that they spend a good deal of time at the funerals of the spouses, friends, and family members who make up the warp and woof of their lives. They describe how a kind of cosmic loneliness sets into their lives. The range and depth of loss varies enormously, but no one escapes it.

Prayer and Ritual

Another important aspect of suffering involves explicit prayer of all kinds. Simple, silent contemplation of the cross brings an ever-deeper awareness of who God is and of who we are. At its best the Christian tradition helps us to rediscover that the cross, like everything else about Jesus, is about being fully and completely human—which means being able to walk in the shoes of our neighbors, especially those who suffer, and experience what it means to be compassionate, to work for the well-being of others. For the poor, the marginalized, and those who suffer, the cross stands as proof of God's tender love and compassion. The cross moves us to nurture compassionate love. For the smug and the comfortable, the cross warns against arrogance, indifference, and empire building.

For me, one of the most powerful prayers related to the suffering of the world is the *Kyrie* of the liturgy with which we began our reflections: "Lord, have mercy. Christ have mercy. Lord have mercy." The Jesus Prayer is an alternate version: "Lord Jesus Christ, son of David, have mercy on me, a sinner." This prayer was whittled down to the mantra "Jesus" by Orthodox monks who recited this word continuously as they walked the land.

Christians are blessed with the Hebrew scriptures as part of their canon. What would Christianity be like without the psalms and their expressions of lament, outrage, complaint, argument, and accusation against God? They also acknowledge the experience of suffering that comes when God seems absent or silent. These prayers take the stark reality of suffering seriously, as in Psalm 88, which ends:

> O Lord, why do you cast me off?
> Why do you hide your face from me? . . .
> You have caused friend and neighbor to shun me;
> my companions are in darkness. (Ps 88:14, 18)

And the familiar words of Psalm 22, which the evangelists placed in Jesus' mouth on the cross:

> "My God, my God,
> why have you forsaken me?" (Ps 22:1)[29]

Other psalms help move disciples from lament to expressions of trust, joy, and confidence that God will rescue them. The saintly pastor of my church prays simply each Sunday, "For those still in harm's way, Lord, hear our prayer."

Hope

It takes a great deal of courage to be hopeful in an age in which we know so much about the suffering of the world. Hope is one of the most counter-cultural stances we can take, a virtue for which we should pray without ceasing. Paul wrote to the Corinthians, "We are afflicted in every way, but not crushed; perplexed, but not driven to despair; persecuted, but not forsaken; struck down, but not destroyed" (2 Cor 4:8–9). For Jesuit theologian Karl Rahner the mysterious identification between Jesus and every human being allows us to say, "Wherever you come across someone who is dying, you find me, the one dying on the cross." We perceive the dying person either as entering into emptiness and nothingness, or into the "sheltering incomprehensibility which we call God."[30] For believers, the cross and resurrection are the guarantee of this sheltering incomprehensibility.

In an Easter homily, Rahner wrote:

> Christ is already in the midst of all the poor things of this earth, which we cannot leave because it is our mother. . . . He is in all tears and in all death as hidden rejoicing and as the life which triumphs by appearing to die. He is in the beggar to whom we give, as the secret wealth which accrues to the donor. He is in the pitiful defeats of his servants, as the victory which is God's alone. He is in our powerlessness as the power which can allow itself to seem weak, because it is unconquerable. He is even in the midst of sin as the mercy of eternal love patient and willing to the end.[31]

Amid the darkness of evil and suffering, the cross stands as a beacon of light. But there is no magic here. Jesus neither seeks a violent death nor is he rescued from death. Nevertheless, so the story of faith goes, new life comes out of death.

Suffering does not have to lead to despair, since the cross tells us that God is alongside us in our pain. The cross tells us that God, in the person of Jesus Christ, has entered fully into human life, learning for himself what it is like to be rejected, ridiculed, and subjected to pain and suffering. Through faith, the cross awakens the realization that historical failure is not the final evidence of what the future holds. The cross stands as a symbol of the hope that is born of resurrection. Prayer and ritual of the cross function to create a new world. Liturgical theologian, Nathan Mitchell, describes the celebration of the cross and resurrection as "a passionate human outcry against extinction; it rebels against the ending of the waltz, the fading of the rose, the dying of the light; it is resistance, rage and rebellion" against the seeming finality of the darkness.[32]

Conclusion

The Christian God takes human suffering seriously and personally enters into it, transforming it from within. The Christian life is built on the conviction that suffering can never be the final word about individual lives or about history. What a tragedy if we never get past "Poor me"; "Grin and bear it"; "Life sucks"; or "Where is the closest euphoric exit?" Suffering is a journey—an aspect of Christian discipleship that can teach us a lot about ourselves, help us mature, and allow us to grow closer to God. We live in a culture that lures us to bypass the journey in favor of the destination: the nearest pill, quick fix, or instant gratification. In this sense the Christian life calls us to be counter-cultural, to stay the course, to take the time to understand, to pray, to open ourselves to God's presence.

When we deny, avoid, repress, or inflict suffering, God understands and continues to embrace us. But these options diminish our passion for life, our ability to enter into the intensity and insight of life's joys. Finding ways to identify, face, and live with our suffering grounds our ability to express our affliction in anguish, anger, pain, and lament. The psalms give voice to these well-worn paths of lament. They help us avoid being destroyed by suffering or swallowed up in self-pity or apathy. In the heart of the dark night we open ourselves to creative forces that lead us away from despair and into the light.

But the mystery of suffering is above all concerned with the mystery of love. Christians do not celebrate the suffering of Jesus but his love, expressed in his willingness to die rather than to live a life without mercy, compassion, and forgiveness. Accepting and trusting God's love—even to death on a cross—empowers us to alleviate suffering wherever we find it and opens our eyes to the possibility that good can come from it. We successfully engage in this process only through the power of the Spirit, who as Gift and Love brings life and courage, humility, and creativity.

Human suffering and the cross of Jesus Christ resist exhaustive interpretation, and surely no generation can dictate the meaning of the cross for another. In each culture the cross will heal, defend, save, protect, free, forgive, and give refuge and life in distinctive ways. Each generation of Christians must attend to human suffering and return to the cross to encounter the Crucified in its own way. What do we think happened there? And what difference does it make for us and for our world? Experienced at the foot of the cross, suffering can become transformed in amazing ways. Against a culture of affluence and death, the Christian story provides a new standard for a meaning of power that begets life even from the desolation of defeat and death. It generates energy to confront the forces of death that surround us, lures us to become more compassionate, and leads us to ritualize its meaning.

The poorest, most marginalized among us are witnesses when they find comfort and companionship with Jesus and embrace the revelation of a God who suffers with and for us, a God who has the power in the end to wipe away every tear (Rv 21:4). African American spirituals provide one of the most vivid testimonies of a suffering and a faith that I, as comfortable "white folk," will never fully understand. Nonetheless, the challenge for all Christians is to experience the cross as a symbol out of which we live, teaching us something important about how we are to be with and for one another. To live the Christian life is to answer the call to "wipe away every tear" as we wait in hope for the final end of suffering. But even more important, we are to live with the knowledge that "there is no alien sorrow"—of the living or the dead. The rescue or the destruction of life is the rescue or destruction of us all.[33]

Julian of Norwich, a fourteenth-century English anchoress, wrote of her visions of the crucified Jesus. Her youthful desire to share in Christ's suffering sustained her throughout her life. In the end she concludes that the meaning of her vision of the Crucified was love. Her years of meditating on her vision of the cross filled her with compassion for all her "even Christians." In the midst of the terrible struggles of the fourteenth century—war, rape, pillage, unjust taxation, and three occurrences of the plague, which decimated the population—Julian sees the cross as the loving gesture of a God who longs to offer comfort and support to those who suffer. Throughout her life, as Julian sees herself reflected in this loving face of God, she becomes a loving, compassionate woman and a confident theologian. She sees joy in God's willingness to suffer as a consequence of his infinite love for the human race and all of creation. Her message is clear—Julian met a God who is no stranger to any suffering the world endures.

As we reflect on our own suffering and reach out to alleviate the suffering of the world, the words of the poet Adam Zagajewski come to mind. He juxtaposes the disfigurement and the simple joys of life:

> Try to praise the mutilated world.
> Remember June's long days,
> and wild strawberries, drops of wine, the dew.
> . . .
> You've seen the refugees heading nowhere,
> . . .
> You should praise the mutilated world.
> . . . .
> And the gray feather a thrush lost,
> And the gentle light that strays and vanishes and
>   returns.[34]

Notes

1. Available on the npr.org website.

2. See davidlangmusic.com.

3. Available on the pacificchorale.org website.

4. See Elizabeth Dreyer, *Earth Crammed with Heaven: A Spirituality of Everyday Life* (Mahwah, NJ: Paulist Press, 1994), 144–46.

5. Joseph F. Kelly, *The Problem of Evil in the Western Tradition: From the Book of Job to Modern Genetics* (Collegeville, MN: The Liturgical Press, 2002), 14.

6. See Elise Saggau, "Dying to Live: A Response to the Mystery of Human Suffering," *Stauros Notebook* 12, no. 4 (Fall 1993). Available on the stauros.arthurcp.org website.

7. Albert C. Outler, "God's Providence and the World's Anguish," in *The Mystery of Suffering and Death*, ed. Michael J. Taylor (Staten Island, NY: Alba House, 1973), 16.

8. James L. Fredericks, "Interreligious Friendship: A New Theological Virtue," *Journal of Ecumenical Studies* 35, no. 2 (Spring 1998): 172.

9. Dietrich Bonhoeffer, *A Testament to Freedom: The Essential Writings of Dietrich Bonhoeffer*, ed. Geffrey B. Kelly and F. Burton Nelson (New York: Harper Collins, 1990, 1995), 508.

10. Richard McBrien, *Catholicism* (San Francisco: HarperSanFrancisco, 1994), 345.

11. Thomas Merton, *No Man Is an Island* (New York: Mariner Books, 2002), 77.

12. To endorse the horrendous suffering of slavery by preaching that suffering is God's will or that it is spiritually desirable is a dramatic betrayal of the gospel. M. Shawn Copeland remarks that Christianity sought to "bind slaves to their condition by inculcating caricatures of the cardinal virtues of patience, long-suffering, forbearance, love, faith and hope." See "'Wading through Many Sorrows': Toward a Theology of Suffering in Womanist Perspective," in *A Troubling in My Soul: Womanist Perspectives on Evil and Suffering*, ed. Emilie M. Townes (Maryknoll, NY: Orbis Books, 1993), 122.

13. A best seller on this topic is Rabbi Harold S. Kushner, *When Bad Things Happen to Good People* (New York: Anchor Press, 2004). Originally published in 1978 by Random House.

14. All biblical quotations are from the New Revised Standard Version (NRSV).

15. For a range of positions, see Douglas John Hall, *God and Human Suffering: An Exercise in the Theology of the Cross* (Minneapolis, MN: Fortress Press, 1987); Gustavo Gutiérrez, *On Job: God-Talk and the Suffering of the Innocent* (Maryknoll, NY: Orbis Books, 1987); Marjorie Suchocki, *The Fall to Violence* (New York: Continuum, 1995); John Thiel, *God, Evil, and Innocent Suffering: A Theological Reflection* (New York: Crossroad, 2002); William Hasker, *The Triumph of God over Evil: Theodicy for a World of Suffering* (Downers Grove, IL: IVP Academic, 2008); and John Hick, *Evil and the God of Love* (New York: Palgrave Macmillan, 2010).

16. See Jaroslav Pelikan, *Jesus Through the Centuries: His Place in the History of Culture* (New Haven, CT: Yale University Press, 1985).

17. John L. McKenzie, "The Son of Man Must Suffer," in *The Mystery of Suffering and Death*, ed. Michael J. Taylor (Staten Island, NY: Alba House, 1973), 40.

18. Cited in Johann M. Vento, "Violence, Trauma, and Resistance: A Feminist Appraisal of Metz's Mysticism of Suffering Unto God," *Horizons* 29, no. 1 (2002): 11.

19. See Cynthia S. W. Crysdale, *Embracing Travail: Retrieving the Cross Today* (New York: Continuum, 1999).

20. Elizabeth A. Dreyer, "Afterword: 'Behold the One You Seek Has Been Lifted Up,'" in *The Cross in Christian Tradition: From Paul to Bonaventure*, ed. Elizabeth A. Dreyer (Mahwah, NJ: Paulist Press, 2000), 248.

21. The work of Elizabeth Johnson is one example, in which the doctrine of God is viewed through the lens of gender. See *Quest for the Living God: Mapping Frontiers in the Theology of God* (New York: Continuum, 2011); idem, *She Who Is: The Mystery of God in Feminist Theological Discourse* (New York: Crossroad, [1992] 2002).

22. McKenzie, "The Son of Man Must Suffer," 42.

23. Saggau, "Dying to Live."

24. McKenzie, "The Son of Man Must Suffer," 37.

25. John Dear, "This Lent, Practice a Spirituality of Resistance," *National Catholic Reporter,* March 8, 2011.

26. Elizabeth A. Dreyer, *Holy Power, Holy Presence: Rediscovering Medieval Metaphors for the Holy Spirit* (Mahwah, NJ: Paulist Press, 2007), 247–50.

27. Constance Fitzgerald, "Impasse and Dark Night," in *Women's Spirituality* 2nd ed., ed. Joann Wolski Conn (New York: Paulist Press, 1996), 410–35.

28. Gail Caldwell, "Regulating Sorrow," *New York Times Book Review*, April 17, 2011.

29. See Mary Catherine Hilkert, "Preaching the Folly of the Cross," *Word and World* 19, no. 1 (Winter 1999): 43.

30. Karl Rahner, *Opportunities for Faith: Elements of a Modern Spirituality*, trans. Edward Quinn (New York: The Seabury Press, 1970), 27.

31. Karl Rahner, "Easter: A Faith That Loves the Earth," in *The Great Church Year*, ed. A. Raffelt, trans. Harvey D. Egan (New York: Crossroad, 1994), 196.

32. Nathan Mitchell, "The Cross That Spoke," in Dreyer, *The Cross in Christian Tradition*, 83–84.

33. Dorothee Soelle, *Suffering*, trans. Everett R. Kalin (Minneapolis, MN: Augsburg Fortress, 1984), 173–74.

34. Adam Zagajewski, "Try to Praise the Mutilated World," trans. Clare Cavanagh, *The New Yorker* (September 24, 2001), 96.

Contributors

Daniel J. Harrington, SJ, professor of New Testament at the Boston College School of Theology and Ministry, is a graduate of Boston College and Harvard University (PhD, 1970). He has served as editor of *New Testament Abstracts* since 1972 and is also editor of the Sacra Pagina series of New Testament commentaries. His research has focused on Second Temple Judaism (including the Dead Sea scrolls) and the relationship between Judaism and early Christianity, as well as the exegesis of the New Testament writings and biblical theology. A past president of the Catholic Biblical Association, he is the author of over fifty books, including *Why Do We Suffer? A Scriptural Approach to the Human Condition* (2000).

M. Dennis Hamm, SJ, a priest of the Society of Jesus since 1970, is professor of theology and holder of the Amelia B. and Emil G. Endowed Faculty Chair in Catholic Theology at Creighton University, where he has taught scripture since 1975 in both the undergraduate and graduate divisions. He holds advanced degrees in English (BS, Marquette, 1958; MA, St. Louis University, 1964), philosophy and letters (PhL, St. Louis University, 1964) and biblical languages and literature (PhD, St. Louis University, 1975). He supplemented these studies as a fellow at Yale School of Divinity (1973–75), a researcher at the Pontifical Biblical Institute, Rome (1985–86), a worker on the Bethsaida dig in Israel (summer of 1988), a scholar-in-residence at the Ecumenical Institute for Cultural Research, Collegeville, Minnesota (1994–95), and at the Tantur Ecumenical Institute, Jerusalem (2001–2). His articles have appeared in *Biblica, The Catholic Biblical Quarterly, The Journal of Biblical Literature, The Journal for the Study of*

the New Testament, The Way, The Bible Today, Church, Worship,
and *America,* and in reference works such as *The Anchor Bible
Dictionary, The New Catholic Encyclopaedia,* and *The Collegeville Pastoral Dictionary of the Bible.* For three years (Novem-
ber of 1996 through October 1999) he wrote the weekly "Word"
column for *America.* These were later published in three volumes
by Liturgical Press under the title *Let the Scriptures Speak: Reflections on the Sunday Readings, Year A, Year B, and Year C.*
The Liturgical Press has published his commentary on the Acts
of the Apostles as part of the new Collegeville Commentary in
the fall of 2005. His most recent book is *Building Our House on
Rock: The Sermon on the Mount as Jesus' Vision for our Lives,
as Told by Matthew and Luke,* from the Word Among Us Press
(2011). A commentary on the prison letters of Paul is forthcoming
from Baker Academic.

Susan A. Calef, PhD, is a New Testament scholar at Creighton
University, where she teaches graduate and undergraduate courses
in New Testament in the Theology Department and in the Christian Spirituality Program. Having served as director of graduate
studies in theology for five years, Dr. Calef is now the director of
women's and gender studies at Creighton. She earned an MA in
biblical literature and languages from Catholic Theological Union
(Chicago), which included studies in Greece, Turkey, and Israel; a
second MA in biblical studies from the University of Notre Dame,
and a PhD in New Testament and Christian origins, also from the
University of Notre Dame. Much of her research has focused on
the roles of women in Pauline communities and on the figure of
Thecla in the *Acts of Paul and Thecla,* an early Christian work
dated to the late second or early third century. Currently, Dr. Calef
is working on two books, one on the Gospel of Mark entitled
Willing Spirit, Weak Flesh: Mark's Spirituality of Discipleship,
and another, a feminist commentary on the Gospel of Mark, for
Liturgical Press. A longer-term book project focuses on the spiritualities of the four Gospels, tentatively entitled *Gospel-Telling:
Narrative Contributions to Christian Spirituality.*

Richard W. Miller has a BA in theology and philosophy from the University of Notre Dame and a MA and PhD in theology from Boston College. He is director of the master's program in theology at Creighton University and is an associate professor of systematic theology at Creighton. He has published in the *Heythrop Journal*, *New Blackfriars*, and the *Journal for Peace and Justice Studies*. He is also a contributor to and editor of six books, including *God, Creation, and Climate Change: A Catholic Response to the Environmental Crisis* (Orbis Books, 2010), which was awarded a Catholic Press Association of the United States and Canada book award (2011).

Michael J. Himes was ordained to the priesthood for the Diocese of Brooklyn in 1972. He was awarded with distinction a PhD in the history of Christianity from the University of Chicago. From 1977 until 1987 he served as dean of the Seminary of the Immaculate Conception in Huntington, New York, and from 1987 until 1993 was associate professor and director of the collegiate program in theology at the University of Notre Dame, whose graduating classes twice voted him their most influential teacher. Currently he is professor of theology at Boston College, where he has been honored with the Phi Beta Kappa Award for excellence in undergraduate teaching. He has been awarded five honorary doctorates and is a recipient of the Social Concerns Medal of the University of Notre Dame and the Washington Theological Union's Sophia Award for Excellence in Theology. He has written or edited six books and has twice been the recipient of the Catholic Press Association Book Award. His articles have appeared in many books and numerous journals here and in England. He has lectured widely in the United States, Canada, Europe, and Australia.

Elizabeth A. Dreyer, PhD, is professor emerita of religious studies at Fairfield University in Fairfield, Connecticut, and adjunct professor of historical theology at Hartford Seminary. She has held appointments at the College of St. Catherine in St. Paul,

Minnesota, The Catholic University of America, and the Washington Theological Union in Washington, DC. She created and edited the award-winning eight-volume series *Called to Holiness: Spirituality for Catholic Women* (Franciscan Media, 2008–10). She is the recipient of the Elizabeth Ann Seton Medal from Mount Saint Joseph's College in Cincinnati, Ohio, awarded to women for outstanding theological contributions in the United States.